Understanding the Human Mind

The Pursuit of Consciousness

Jason Browne

© **Copyright 2020 - All rights reserved.**

The content contained within this book may not be reproduced, duplicated or transmitted without direct written permission from the author or the publisher.

Under no circumstances will any blame or legal responsibility be held against the publisher, or author, for any damages, reparation, or monetary loss due to the information contained within this book, either directly or indirectly.

Legal Notice:

This book is copyright protected. It is only for personal use. You cannot amend, distribute, sell, use, quote or paraphrase any part, or the content within this book, without the consent of the author or publisher.

Disclaimer Notice:

Please note the information contained within this document is for educational and entertainment purposes only. All effort has been executed to present accurate, up to date, reliable, complete information. No warranties of any kind are declared or implied. Readers acknowledge that the author is not engaged in the rendering of legal, financial, medical or professional advice. The content within this book has been derived from various sources. Please consult a licensed professional before attempting any techniques outlined in this book.

By reading this document, the reader agrees that under no circumstances is the author responsible for any losses, direct or indirect, that are incurred as a result of the use of the information contained within this document, including, but not limited to, errors, omissions, or inaccuracies.

Table of Contents

INTRODUCTION 1

**CHAPTER 1: THE EVOLUTION OF THE HUMAN MIND—
NATURE'S GREATEST ACCOMPLISHMENT** 7

THE BIOLOGICAL EVOLUTION COMPONENT 8
THE ANATOMY OF THE BRAIN AND HIGHER FUNCTIONING 12
THE CONSCIOUSNESS DEBATE 22

**CHAPTER 2: METAPHYSICS OF CONSCIOUSNESS—
UNDERSTANDING WHY AND HOW WE ARE SELF-CONSCIOUS**
.... 25

THE THEORIES BEHIND CONSCIOUSNESS 26
  Dualism versus Materialism 27
  Neural Theory 30
  Representational Theories 30
  Multiple Drafts Model 32
  Global Workspace Theory 33
  An Overview 34

**CHAPTER 3: NEUROSCIENCE—ONE STEP CLOSER TO
UNDERSTANDING CONSCIOUSNESS** 37

THE NEUROSCIENCE OF CONSCIOUSNESS 38

**CHAPTER 4: PSYCHOLOGY OF CONSCIOUSNESS—HEAL THE
MIND THROUGH SCIENCE** 47

CONSCIOUSNESS AND PSYCHOLOGY 48
NEUROPSYCHOLOGY 55
CONSCIOUSNESS IN THERAPY 58

**CHAPTER 5: SPIRITUALITY AND CONSCIOUSNESS—THE
PROMISE OF A HIGHER AWARENESS** 63

How Spirituality Fits into the Pursuit of Consciousness 64

CHAPTER 6: ALTERED STATES OF CONSCIOUSNESS 73

Yoga.. *74*
Native American Dance *76*
Voodoo *78*
Hypnosis *78*
Holotropic Approaches *79*
Psychedelics *80*
Choosing a Method of Altering Consciousness 84

CHAPTER 7: A SIMPLE GUIDE TO A HIGHER STATE OF CONSCIOUSNESS 87

Simple Steps to Achieving Higher Consciousness 88

CHAPTER 8: THE BIGGER QUESTION: CONSCIOUSNESS AND THE DILEMMA OF CHOICE 111

CONCLUSION 115

REFERENCES 121

Introduction

"Our world is in crisis because of the absence of consciousness" - Terence McKenna

Since the dawn of time and the moment we became aware of our surroundings and our interactions with it, the human species has sought to answer questions around our consciousness. The manner in which our consciousness is defined has varied throughout the ages, but today we understand it as our individual awareness of our own thoughts, feelings, memories, sensations, and environment. If we are aware of ourselves and the fact that the world around us exists, then we have consciousness. The word is, of course, also used as a medical term for a state in which a person is awake but, essentially, the term seeks to determine the same thing: if a person has awareness of the self and the environment, they have consciousness.

No two forms of consciousness are the same, though, and the make-up of each individual's consciousness is unique to their own experiences. Our human experience is the filter through which our individual consciousness forms and is what makes each of us unique. As society began to develop this concept of consciousness, simply knowing its definition was not enough. We began to study, research, and debate the concept and all its facets.

The connection, or possible lack thereof, between the mind and the body has always been a major point of contention and will likely continue to be for some time. Some prefer to think of our mind and body as separate entities while others prefer the idea that one is able to influence the other. As a society, we have pivoted quite significantly and repeatedly over the ages between believing that there is no division between the mind and body and the insistence that each is its own entity. The connection between our consciousness and our physical brain has also been explored. Many prefer to believe that consciousness simply exists and does not need a physical structure in order to do so, while others balk at the idea and insist that there is no way that thinking and feeling can happen without a container. At one point, the debate almost fizzled to an end but it was quickly revived by those who simply could not fathom never knowing the answers to the questions.

We have asked and, without a doubt, continue to ask where our consciousness actually 'lives.' Is it a part of our brain, and, if so, how is it possible that people report having a form of awareness in the period between death and resuscitation when, essentially, the brain should no longer be functioning? Of course, the answer to this question will always depend on who you ask as scientists will say that the moment the brain ceases to function the part of you that is aware also no longer exists. While we are on the topic, it is interesting to note that brain cells continue to fire off electrical signals for quite some time after death. People approaching the matter from a more spiritual perspective will say that consciousness is part of your soul, and therefore continues on whether there is a body to house it or not. In this book, we will explore all of these possibilities but most importantly, we will try to determine exactly what an ordinary person like you or I can do to live in a higher state of consciousness. The world needs us to do this and then, in turn, it needs us to encourage others to do the same so that every tiny advancement will put us closer to being happier, kinder, and more empathetic as a species.

In *Understanding the Human Mind*, I would like to explore all of these avenues and then arrive at a reconciliation of the two so that we can all move on with a better understanding of not just exactly where consciousness lives but how we can use it to be better human beings. As our introductory quotation to this section suggests, perhaps the crises we are seeing in the world today, of all varieties, have at the root of them one single cause: a lack of consciousness.

While the idea of truly understanding our awareness of the world, its fluidity, and how we can use the concept to improve ourselves may sound exciting, be aware that it also comes with great responsibility. The more we understand, the less we can ignore. The deeper we dig, the greater possibility that we will uncover things about ourselves and our environment that make us uncomfortable.

Your interest in this subject, though, and your willingness to delve deeper into understanding it suggests that you would be okay with being taken out of your comfort zone. It is impossible to study anything related to the human psyche without comparing the concepts we learn to our own experience. This comparison can sometimes be difficult, but it will always be valuable. Don't be afraid to be honest and truthful with yourself as you read this book. That really is the only way you are going to gain real value from it.

If you seek to truly understand how consciousness is formed, grows, changes, and persists, then many of your questions will be answered in *Understanding the Human Mind*. There will remain questions that only you can answer, though, and that will be a journey that continues for you long after you turn the final page of this book. I will teach you what I have learned about consciousness in general, but you will need to apply that to your unique situation, and, perhaps, that will be the most revealing part of all. It is likely our unique individuality that has caused us to never really find an answer to the question of consciousness because in doing so we would be asking, "Who am I?" The wonderful thing that happens when we are brave enough to start asking that question, though, is that we start finding answers that we didn't know were there, and then we start asking more questions. These questions and answers don't necessarily elevate our level of consciousness but they certainly make us better human beings than we were before. So if you are ready to start asking questions and seeking answers, get your consciousness cap on.

As we move into the body of this book, let us reconsider the quote we opened with. Is the situation we find ourselves in really as a result of a lack of consciousness? Or is it perhaps as a result of a lack of understanding of consciousness? Can we improve our own world simply by seeking answers? If yes, then we are about to begin the most prolific of journeys.

Chapter 1:

The Evolution of the Human Mind—Nature's Greatest Accomplishment

So how did consciousness actually develop? Was it always there and we just don't have a written record of it, or did it grow incrementally through each twist of evolution? If the latter is the case and our consciousness evolved with us then why did we need it in the first place? Why and how did we leave the Ape Man behind and develop intelligence and consciousness beyond that of our ancient ancestors? In this chapter, we will seek to answer all of these questions. We will delve into the actual evolutionary process that we believe saw the dawn of consciousness and look at which parts of the brain and nervous system had to develop in order for us to have these experiences.

Although this chapter is focused on the medical, scientific, and evolutionary aspects of consciousness, it is important for us to already begin asking questions that we seek to answer. Reading and considering the information we provide here will give you a richer experience of this book. Do not simply accept the information provided but rather question it and seek answers, and if something resonates with you, then ask yourself why it does. Although you may not realize it, you already have a preconception of what consciousness is, and, as human beings do, you are simply seeking validation for your theory. Allow yourself to be challenged by the information that follows and deeply question your own personal beliefs. We all attach ourselves to one or another theory or school of thought. If you are a very analytical thinker, then the information in this chapter will likely resonate with you. If you are a deeply spiritual or religious person, then you may find yourself having difficulty with some of the concepts here. Do not allow yourself to simply seek information that qualifies your existing beliefs. If you feel uncomfortable when reading a specific theory, delve into those feelings and allow them to grow within you. This book is not presented as a magical solution to the question of consciousness. Rather, it is an amalgamation of the various schools of thought and a trigger for you to form your own belief.

The Biological Evolution Component

What do you think of when you picture the starting point of mankind? This picture will be different for everyone depending on the mindset that you are approaching the question from. In this chapter, we approach this picture from the perspective of the theory of evolution and the historical evidence that relates to it. The picture that originally formed in your mind, though, should not be disregarded. As human beings in a modern world, we find it difficult to comprehend that people who lived differently from us could be equally conscious, if not more so. For some, we correlate the availability of information with consciousness, so we assume that a person living in a cave with no access to modern amenities couldn't possibly have the same level of consciousness as we do. Of course, this is a misconception, and as we get into the evolution of the concept of consciousness, it is perhaps important to keep in mind that we may be less conscious today than we ever have been in the history of mankind.

Scientific research tells us that from the beginning of life on earth the animals and organisms that existed had the cellular capability to communicate. This communication consisted primarily of electrical impulses and chemical signals, much like what happens with hormones and synapses firing in our human bodies today, and some organisms have never evolved beyond that place. From that point, though, it was never going to be a huge leap for cells to become specialized message carriers. When these cells began to form, they promulgated what we now refer to as the nervous system, although initially, it was in a very primitive form.

From this point of the development of a primitive nervous system, both our environment and evolution started to act together in order to develop this message carrying system into the complex system we know today.

About 200 million years ago the first mammals had a structure in their brain called the neocortex. This structure consists of several additional layers of neural tissue within the brain and it allows for movement past rudimentary and base survival behavior, and instead promotes complex and flexible actions. It is this structure of the brain that provided mammals with the ability to begin enacted behaviors which would take them from simply existing through eating, sleeping, and procreating, to living complex lives, regardless of species. As mammals began to develop social behaviors such as living in groups and having hierarchies within their groups, the neocortex developed even further. The group of mammals that exhibited this advancement most distinctly were primates and as their own social structures developed, the neocortex incrementally increased in size with each generation and gained a greater supply of neural connections. This neocortex development allowed primates to further integrate and more deeply process information that they received from their environment. No longer did they only have thoughts around survival but rather, they developed the ability to think in abstract ways.

As abstract thinking began to develop in primates, their brains were capable of processing more incoming information. They were also able to start identifying and seeking out patterns in information that became as real to their thought process as physical items that they could touch. As the neocortex expanded, primates began to develop into Homosapiens as the body evolved to meet the growing needs of the brain and the increasing awareness of the world around it. Homosapiens developed tools, learned how to harness fire, and constructed forms of verbal communication in speech. Within very little comparative time, we began to understand how we existed within the space around us, we developed a concept of time passing, and began to understand the eventuality of death. Soon, we were able to question the reason for our existence and start to seek purpose.

The dawn of consciousness brought with it a deep need to understand where this consciousness really comes from and what its components are. This speculation has been ongoing over thousands of years in different forms and, while we have made great strides in understanding, most of what we know is based on speculation and a wide range of beliefs. While we can put average dates on when we believe the debate around consciousness began, it is important to consider the role of language and written record in this assumption. Do we assume that there was no debate or awareness of consciousness simply because language as we see it today and written records did not predate a specific point in time? While we may have an idea of how and roughly when consciousness formed, we cannot assume that no other form of consciousness existed before that point either.

The Anatomy of the Brain and Higher Functioning

In order for us to understand the concept of consciousness, we must first perhaps understand the structure and functioning of the organ in which some think consciousness resides—the brain.

In the average human being, the brain weighs around three pounds. It controls all of the functions of our body, interprets information from the outside world, and if the science is to be believed, it embodies the essence of the mind and the soul. The brain governs creativity, intelligence, memory, and emotion, among other cognitive processes. Its main structures are the cerebellum, cerebrum, and the brainstem, and it is contained within the skull which forms a protective layer to prevent damage. The brain constantly receives information from our five senses and then assembles the information into a message that will have meaning for us. The brain is a component of the central nervous system which also includes the spinal cord. Each structure in the brain has a different function, some with crossover and some completely independent of the others.

The cerebrum is the largest part of the brain and is made up of two hemispheres. It controls higher functions like the interpretation of vision, touch, hearing, speech, emotions, reasoning, the fine control of movement, and learning functions.

The cerebellum is located underneath the cerebrum. It coordinates the movements of muscles and helps to maintain balance and posture.

The brainstem functions as a relay center between the two aforementioned structures and the spinal cord. The brainstem controls automatic functions that we do not need to consciously control like heart rate, breathing, body temperature, the wake and sleep cycle, sneezing, digestion, vomiting, coughing, and swallowing.

The two hemispheres of the cerebrum are connected by a bundle of fibers called the corpus callosum. These fibers transmit messages from one side of the brain to the other. Each hemisphere of the brain controls the opposite side of the body (i.e., the left hemisphere controls the right side of the body, and vice versa). This becomes evident when damage occurs to one side of the brain and loss of function is seen in the opposite side of the body. You will likely have come across the suggestion that some people are "left-brained" and some people are "right-brained." This idea is not entirely unscientific. While all human beings use both sides of their brain, there does seem to be evidence that some individuals use one side more than the other. The functions that are controlled in either hemisphere are then more pronounced in that individual.

The left hemisphere of the brain, for instance, controls comprehension, speech, arithmetic, and writing, while the right hemisphere controls spatial ability, creativity, artistic talents, and musical skills. Depending on your nature, you may be more left-brained (analytical), or you may be more right-brained (creative). Most individuals have a mix of both talents, and it is entirely possible for a predominantly right-brained person, for instance, to develop their left-brain use, consciously, through practice.

The two distinct hemispheres are further divided into four lobes each. These lobes are called the parietal, occipital, temporal, and frontal lobes. None of the structures of the brain operate independently, and each is in constant and complex contact with the other areas of the brain. The four lobes have specified functions to perform which include:

- **Parietal:** language use and interpretation, interpretation of pain, heat, cold, and touch, spatial and visual perceptions, and the interpretations of signals from hearing, vision, motor, memory, and sensory perceptions.
- **Occipital:** interpretation of vision including light, color, and movement.
- **Temporal:** the understanding of language, hearing, memory, sequencing, and organization.
- **Frontal:** behavior, emotions, personality, planning, problem-solving, judgment, speech, writing, concentration, intelligence, and self-awareness.

The neocortex is the outer layer of the cerebrum and, since this is the part of the brain that developed as our cognitive abilities or consciousness did, it makes sense that the cerebrum would be responsible for the functions that it is. Interestingly, the mammal with the most developed neocortex is not a human being, it is a species of dolphin called the long-finned pilot whale. If the development of the neocortex is directly related to consciousness, then this should certainly make us wonder what this species of dolphin is capable of if their neocortex is more developed than ours. The cerebrum is sometimes referred to as "the seat of consciousness" due to the fact that so many high-level intellectual functions take place in this structure.

Pathways referred to as white matter tracts serve to connect areas of the cortex to one another. Messages can travel between lobes, gyruses, sides of the brain, and between structures that are located deep in the brain.

The hypothalamus is at the bottom of the third ventricle and controls the autonomic system. It controls behaviors like sleep, thirst, hunger, and sexual response. It also helps to regulate emotions, body temperature, blood pressure, and secretion of hormones.

The pituitary gland is located in a small groove of bone at the base of the skull called the sella turcica. This gland is connected to the hypothalamus via the pituitary stalk. It is known as the "master gland," and it regulates all other endocrine glands in the body. It releases hormones that promote bone and muscle growth, control sexual development, and our stress response.

The pineal gland is behind the third ventricle. It regulates the Circadian clock, also known as our internal clock, and the rhythms of this clock through the secretion of melatonin. It also plays a small role in sexual development.

The thalamus acts as a relay station for the messages and signals that come and go to the cortex. It facilitates alertness and memory, pain sensations, and attention.

The basal ganglia is made up of the putamen, caudate, and globus pallidus. This group of nuclei works together with the cerebellum to coordinate fine motor actions, like the movement of the fingertips.

The limbic system is our emotional center, as well as the center for learning, and memory. The system is composed of the hypothalamus, cingulate gyri, and hippocampus.

The left hemisphere of the brain is responsible for speech and language and is referred to as the 'dominant' hemisphere. The right hemisphere works to help us interpret spatial processing and visual information. In about one-third of left-handed people, the function of speech may be controlled by the right side of the brain. People who are left-handed may need special testing to determine the location of their speech center if surgery in that area is ever required.

A disturbance of language affecting comprehension, production of speech, writing, or reading due to brain injury is called aphasia. This will most commonly result from trauma or a stroke. The location of damage in the brain will determine the type of aphasia.

- **Broca's area** is situated in the left frontal lobe. If damage is experienced in this area, there may be difficulty moving the facial muscles or tongue to produce the sounds we need to form speech. The person will still be able to understand spoken language and read but have difficulty with writing and speaking. An example would be a person who cannot form letters or combine letters to make words or a child that does not fit their writing between the lines. This is called Broca's Aphasia.
- **Wernicke's area** is situated in the left temporal lobe. When damage occurs to this area, Wernicke's aphasia results. The person may add unnecessary words, create new words, and speak in long sentences that have no meaning. People suffering from Wernicke's aphasia are able to make speech sounds, but they have difficulty understanding speech, and they are therefore not aware of their mistakes.

The process of memory is a complex one that includes three phases: encoding, storing, and recalling. Different types of memories are formed and recalled from different areas of the brain. In order for an event to move from your short-term to your long-term memory, your brain has to be paying attention and rehearsing the recall; this is called encoding. Working memory or short-term memory emanates in the prefrontal cortex. It stores information for approximately 60 seconds, and its capacity is limited to about seven separate items. For instance, your short-term memory allows you to be able to dial a phone number that someone has just given to you. It also means that you can remember sentences in sequence while reading so that each successive sentence makes sense.

Long-term memory processing happens in the temporal lobe's hippocampus. It is activated when you need to remember something for a longer period. Long-term memory has unlimited duration and content capacity. It allows us to recall personal memories, facts, and figures.

Skill memory emanates in the cerebellum of the brain. This structure transmits information to the basal ganglia in order to store automatic-learned memories such as playing an instrument, tying your shoelaces, or riding a bicycle.

Ventricles which are hollow fluid-filled cavities also form part of the brain. Inside the ventricles exists the choroid plexus which is a ribbon-like structure producing clear and colorless cerebrospinal fluid. Cerebrospinal fluid flows around and inside the spinal cord and brain and cushions it from injury. This fluid is constantly being absorbed and replenished. Deep within the cerebral hemispheres, there are two ventricles referred to as the lateral ventricles. The lateral ventricles both connect through a separate opening called the foramen of Monro, with the third ventricle. This ventricle then forms a connection with the fourth ventricle via the aqueduct of Sylvius, which is a narrow tube. Cerebrospinal fluid flows from the fourth ventricle into the subarachnoid space in order to bathe and cushion the brain. Cerebrospinal fluid is absorbed and then recycled by arachnoid villi in the superior sagittal sinus. Through this absorption and recycling process, a balance is maintained in the amount of cerebrospinal fluid that is produced. A build-up of cerebrospinal fluid can occur if there is a blockage or disruption in this system. This can cause an enlargement of the ventricles or a collection of fluid in the spinal cord.

The skull is present to protect the brain from damage and injury. It is composed of eight bones that are fused together along suture lines. These bones include two parietal bones, two temporal bones, the frontal bone, the sphenoid bone, the occipital bone, and the ethmoid bone. An additional 14 paired bones form the face which includes the zygoma, the maxilla, palatine, lacrimal, nasal, mandible, inferior nasal conchae, and vomer. On the interior of the skull, we find three separate areas: the posterior fossa, anterior fossa, and middle fossa. The location of a tumor is sometimes referred to by these locations. All the veins, arteries, and nerves exit the skull base through holes called foramina, this is similar to cables coming out the back of a computer. The big hole in the middle is where the spinal cord exits.

Communication with the body occurs through twelve pairs of cranial nerves and the spinal cord. Ten of the cranial nerve pairs originate in the brainstem and they control facial sensations, taste, hearing, swallowing, eye movement, and movement of the face, neck, tongue, and shoulder muscles. The cranial nerves that control smell and vision originate in the cerebrum.

The spinal cord and brain are protected and covered by layers of tissue called meninges. From the innermost layer outward they are: the pia mater, the arachnoid mater, and the dura mater.

- The **dura mater** presents as a strong, thick membrane and it closely lines the interior of the skull. It consists of two layers, the meningeal dura and the periosteal, that are fused and separate only to form gaps for veins.
- The **arachnoid mater** presents as a thin, web-like membrane, and it covers the entire brain. It is made up of elastic tissue. The space between the two aforementioned membranes is called the subdural space.
- The **pia mater** envelopes the surface of the brain along all of its grooves and folds. This membrane has many blood vessels reaching deep into the brain.

So how exactly do all of the structures and functions of the brain make any difference in a discussion about consciousness? Well, most theories that we will address in this book focus on some form of imagery or sensory perception and how those elements combine to form our consciousness. If we understand exactly how the brain is structured and which part of the brain controls which functions, it will be far easier for us to understand the philosophies that follow in later chapters.

An interesting discovery has been made by scientists working on the Human Brain Project. The first direct correlation has been discovered between intelligence levels and the size of brain cells. The discovery shows that people who tested at higher intelligence levels also had larger brain neurons, and the electrical signal with which they fire do so at a higher speed than people who tested at average or lower intelligence. A team of Dutch scientists studied 46 patients who were headed for brain tumor removal surgery or surgery to relieve epilepsy. They conducted an IQ test on each of the participants before their surgery. In order to access the part of the brain which was diseased, brain surgeons often have to remove small parts of the temporal lobe which are undamaged. Scientists on this project used that removed healthy tissue to compare its activity and the size of the cells to the IQ scores gleaned from the tests. This is when this correlation was discovered (Human Brain Project, 2018).

The Consciousness Debate

Despite a myriad of explanations, the debate still rages on about what exactly consciousness is. Some believe it to mean that one is actively engaged with the sensory information that is being received and, therefore, one is aware of one's surroundings, feelings, thoughts, and sensations. This belief is a basic definition that in order to have consciousness, we must be awake and aware. Other groups believe that consciousness relies on the firing off of a large number of neurons in the brain. Those who take a more spiritual slant argue that consciousness is not dependent on any anatomical feature and that it is something that exists before we are born and after we die. Still others believe that consciousness does not belong to an individual, and is, instead, something that we are tapping into that belongs to all of mankind.

While it seems unlikely that we will ever have one single understanding of consciousness that fits the beliefs of all, it is certainly possible for us to test the various philosophies for the likelihood of each, and thereby, reach some conclusion of which amalgamation of theories may be the closest to the truth.

Art is another arena in which consciousness seems to play an interesting role. After all, how is it possible that cave paintings have such similar imagery to paintings by Pablo Picasso when the two people painting the art lived millennia apart and should have shared no common consciousness? How is it that, despite the very different world we live in today, books and poems have very similar themes to those written hundreds of years ago?

Philosophers and scientists have been debating the question of what makes human beings more than pieces of complex machinery for centuries. In 1994, in Tucson Arizona, a little-known philosopher called David Chalmers stood in front of an auditorium of people to give a talk on consciousness. The theme of his talk, according to an article in *The Guardian*, was the very 'unscientific' notion that consciousness is what it's like to be inside your own head or even less-scientifically, the concept of the soul. Although he would have no idea at the time, Chalmers was about to reignite the consciousness debate between philosophers and scientists by bringing attention to one of the central mysteries of life and, by doing so, reveal how far any of us are from solving the mystery.

The conference, which took place at the University of Arizona, was rather forward-thinking for its time, and despite risking their reputations, many scientists attended. Chalmers started his speech by discussing the types of questions about the brain that kept scientists busy but which were easily answered by studies and research. These included the science behind how we store memories, how we know to pull our hand away from hot water, and how you can recognize your name across the noise of a party. Chalmers' question to the crowd sparked a different kind of conversation around consciousness—why do we expect all of the processes that make up the brain to actually feel like anything? Why are they not just processes in the same way that a computer has ongoing processes and programs running? Furthermore he asked how an organ—our brain—would be capable of creating the experience of *being*?

Decades after this conference, the debate rages on and we have had an additional element added to the mix—artificial intelligence. Suddenly we have started to ask questions about consciousness as it relates to inanimate objects, and yet, we still have not answered this very question about ourselves.

Chapter 2:

Metaphysics of Consciousness— Understanding Why and How We Are Self-Conscious

Now that we understand the evolutionary process by which we arrived at a state of consciousness, let us see what we can uncover by exploring some of the early philosophies around consciousness.

One of the most important and perplexing areas of philosophy is the quest to explain the nature of consciousness, but the idea remains notoriously ambiguous. The noun 'consciousness' is not often used on its own in contemporary literature, but it is originally derived from the Latin *con* (with) and *scire* (to know). One of the most frequently-used contemporary ideas of a conscious mental state is put forward by Thomas Nagel's famous "what it is like" theory. He says that when he is in a conscious mental state, there is something *it is like* for him to be in that state from his internal point of view. In other words, there should be something for him to compare his own consciousness to. The understanding of this, though, is quite a different matter. For instance, how is that mental state related to the body? Does brain activity explain consciousness? What makes a mental state conscious? The question of consciousness is arguably the most central one in the philosophy of mind. The issue is also closely related to some major metaphysics topics in metaphysics, like the belief in free will, and the possibility of immortality.

The Theories Behind Consciousness

Before we address the theories that have formed around consciousness, let's consider, for a moment, the types of questions that we have sought to answer around the subject.

- Can consciousness ever be explained from a mechanistic viewpoint?
- Does non-human consciousness exist?

- If non-human consciousness does exist, how can we recognize it?
- How does consciousness relate to language, if at all?
- Can consciousness be understood without rendering it down to a division between the mental and the physical elements?
- Would it be possible for computers or robots to gain consciousness?

There are various theories that try to answer these questions.

Dualism versus Materialism

The theory of dualism states that the body and the mind are two separate entities. Dualists deny that the mind exists only as a result of the brain. The dualism school of thought can be further divided into specific ideals including substance dualism which purports that the mind and the body are composed of different types of substances and that the mind is not a 'thing' with physical dimensions or made up of biological matter. Substance dualist beliefs range from the idea that the mind and body affect each other, to the idea that any interaction is only based on the influence of a higher power, as well as the belief that events in the body can affect the mind, but that the mind has no power over the body.

Dualism is the theory that two things exist: the physical world and the mind. Therefore, according to dualism, humans are also made up of two things, the body and the mind. There are several blank spaces and many remaining questions when we contemplate the theory of dualism. Most importantly, it doesn't provide any information about how the mind and body link together to form a human being. The theory of dualism cannot tell us anything concrete about the mind, other than the fact that it exists and works with the body. Dualism argues that the mind encompasses emotion, reason, and consciousness. Machines, which do not have minds, have already shown some level of reasoning, so can this simplistic explanation really offer a valuable standpoint? Brain chemicals have been linked with emotions and the former are physical entities. Consciousness can be impacted by physical things like caffeine, anesthetics, and a blow to the head. So emotion, reason, and consciousness can easily be linked to the physical brain, but this reasoning does not make as much sense when we attribute it to the unknown workings of the mind in a non-physical state.

Property dualists believe that the mental state only exists due to a condition of the brain and, therefore, consciousness occurs as a result of a set of conditions in the brain. Property dualists believe that something cannot exist as a standalone entity if it does not have the attributes of physical matter; therefore, consciousness must just be a property of the physical matter which is the brain. According to the property dualism view, the world is made up of just matter.

Matter has different kinds of properties including those we regard as solely physical, like charge, mass, and the like, and then it has other kinds of properties, like consciousness, that are solely mental.

Idealism, on the other hand, believes that consciousness is the origin of everything material, and, if we did not have consciousness, the material world would not exist for us. This is rather similar to the school of thought of materialism which believes that the mind and the brain are the same thing and that consciousness solely exists as a result of neural activity. Idealism is the view that consciousness is a fundamental feature of reality. The theory goes further by arguing that consciousness is the only component of reality. Philosophers such as Kant, Leibniz, Hegel, Berkeley, Bradley, and Mill have all been champions of idealistic views of consciousness historically. Although the history of idealism is rather complex and many different variants of the theory can be identified, it still has its defenders, and we may be seeing a resurgence in interest around the theory.

In summary, dualism can make it hard to distinguish between mind and body. In materialism, though, the approach is more straightforward, as everything is physical. What's more, the brain's effect on our emotions, decisions, and conscious thought is not in dispute. This means that as far as these theories are concerned, everything can be attributed to neurotransmitters and chemicals in the brain, and we would not assign them to a separate unknown state. Additionally, evolution is a concept based around physical processes, and it therefore makes more sense in an evolutionary context for physicality to be the only accepted entity. Materialism argues that all forms of life evolved from only physical materials by means of a solely physical process, so in this theory, it makes sense that there would not also be a non-physical mind. Also, if the mind did exist, it would be connected to the brain and the processes that occur within the brain, and as a result, those two would not be distinguishable from one another. If this were the case, then the mind would be a redundant entity.

As a result of the concepts of dualism and materialism, several theories around consciousness have emerged.

Neural Theory

The basic premise of this theory is that consciousness comes into being when the neurons in the brain begin to fire within specific ranges. Essentially, this theory states that there is no consciousness before brain activity at a specific level begins and that consciousness ceases to exist after brain activity at that level stops. We will delve deeper into this theory in chapter 3.

Representational Theories

This theory reduces consciousness to a series of activities occurring within the brain and how we perceive those activities. Representational theorists believe that consciousness is merely a representation of the images the brain is seeing and it is shaped by our perception of those images. This theory classifies the states of consciousness into intentional states and phenomenal states. An intentional state is when we create a representation of the mental image of an object by directing our attention to it, and a phenomenal state is caused by a phenomenon outside of our control such as pain or the experience of color. The sum of these two types of states is said to make up consciousness. Within this group of theories, there are three subset schools of thought:

1. First-order representationalism
2. Higher-order representationalism
3. Hybrid representationalism

First-order representationalism attempts to explain consciousness in terms of world-directed intentional states. This sub-theory states that all of the experiences that make up our consciousness are based on the information that the world is giving us and that we cannot separate our experience from that information. In terms of first-order thinking, we do not have any experience that is not formed by information we receive from the outside world. The argument is that this is true even for hallucinations, itches, and pain as these are representations of images we have seen before and signals from our organs.

Higher-order representationalism explains consciousness by linking our awareness of an object or experience to the validity of its existence. In other words, consciousness only comes into being, and objects and experiences only exist, due to our awareness of them.

Hybrid representationalism, as the name suggests, is a combination of the two aforementioned types of representationalism. This version is becoming increasingly popular and states that the psychological state of a human being is part of an overall, more complex state of consciousness.

Multiple Drafts Model

The Multiple Drafts Model aims to guard against the notion that there is a specific place within the brain where consciousness is born. This model purports that the brain is constantly emitting various 'draft' thoughts, experiences, and perceptions, and as we receive more information from our senses or other parts of the brain, these drafts are updated into one final experience of awareness. The Multiple Drafts Model does not see the self as an inner being but rather as a product of an ongoing and changing narrative. This theory gives credence to the fact that consciousness is fluid, open to change, and malleable, and by the same token so is the self. The Multiple Drafts Model argues that recording something in memory is critical for consciousness. The model purports that there is no conscious experience independent of the effects of various vehicles of content. The Multiple Drafts Model further argues that the brain does not bother constructing representations to fill in any blanks in consciousness as that would be a waste of time. So, instead, it continues on with other tasks.

According to the model, we experience a variety of sensory inputs from a specific event and also a variety of interpretations of these inputs. The sensory inputs are present in the brain and then interpreted at different times, so a single event can give rise to a wide range of interpretations, which become much like multiple drafts of a story that is written. As soon as each interpretation is completed, it becomes available to the brain to trigger a related behavior. As is the case with a number of other theories, the Multiple Drafts Model understands conscious experience as occurring over time, as the various interpretations do not instantaneously become available in the mind. This theory, though, denies any clear boundary that separates conscious experiences from all other brain processes. The Multiple Drafts Model states that consciousness is to be found in the flows of information and actions from place to place, rather than some single view. There is also no individual who is able to claim that their particular draft of consciousness is the correct one.

Global Workspace Theory

This theory is one of the most popular among psychologists, and it states that consciousness is formed by the brain extracting pieces of information from an ongoing supply in a "global broadcast network." The theory assumes that our consciousness exists because of an ongoing selection of information by the brain and the nervous system. Global Workspace Theory resembles the idea of working memory and is proposed to correlate with a subjectively experienced event in our working memory which is our inner domain in which we can repeat telephone numbers to ourselves or in which we live out the narrative of our lives. Working memory is usually thought to include visual imagery and inner speech. The theory can be explained in terms of a theater metaphor. In the theater of our consciousness, a *spotlight* of attention will reveal the contents of consciousness. There are *actors* moving on and off stage, delivering speeches or interacting with each other. The *audience* is in the dark (our unconscious). Behind the stage, also not illuminated, are the director (the executive processes in our brain), script writers, stagehands, and scene designers. These processes shape the visible activities in the area of the theater that is illuminated, but they are not visible.

An Overview

Although all of these philosophies make attempts to understand the nature of conscious thought, many questions remain. There is also a large amount of valid criticism for many of the theories as most fail to answer fundamental questions about the purpose of consciousness, and what it can do for us on a personal level. In the chapters that follow, we will attempt to close the gap between these theories and these unanswered questions. We will approach the question of consciousness from a psychological viewpoint and look at how psychotherapists have developed treatments for mental illness and cognitive difficulties by building on some of these theories.

On the other end of the spectrum—although in reality the ideas are not that far apart—is the spiritual aspect of consciousness, which can be no less ignored than scientific data. Through various esoteric practices such as yoga, mindfulness training, and meditation, we also seek to elevate our consciousness to a higher state of awareness. Despite the rooting of these practices in spiritualism, they have scientifically measurable benefits from both a psychological and physical standpoint. We will also delve deeper into the spiritual approach to consciousness later in the book and show how these approaches are useful even if you have no particular spiritual or religious belief system.

Chapter 3:

Neuroscience—One Step Closer to Understanding Consciousness

Consciousness is a topic that is quite significantly studied, and, in recent years, neuroscience has come much closer than ever before to closing the gap between body and mind. As we focused in-depth on the anatomy of the brain in order to understand exactly where the various types of content which make up consciousness emanate, so we must understand the processes that contribute to the content. Some may argue that neuroscience is the only component of consciousness and that our questions can only be answered by examining neural activity. This view may be simplistic, though, as we have quite a significant amount of empirical evidence around brain activity and yet, we still have questions.

As conscious experience in humans depends on brain activity, neuroscience must contribute to the explanation of consciousness. In order to bridge the gap between consciousness and the brain, we need computational and psychological models, neural data, and philosophical analysis so that we can identify the principles that connect brain activity to conscious experience.

The Neuroscience of Consciousness

Neuroscience researchers have studied the various stages of human consciousness and the differences in perception levels in order to understand exactly how the body produces conscious awareness. Researchers have focused on sets of neurons and series of events within those neurons called Neural Correlates of Consciousness (NCC). NCCs are said to be necessary for conscious perception, but they have been found to be parallel and sometimes redundant, which has made pinpointing the exact brain activity related to the formation of consciousness difficult. The definition of NCCs stresses the *minimal* attribute because clearly the entire brain is sufficient to give rise to consciousness. The question is which of the brain's subcomponents are essential to produce conscious experience? As an example, it is likely that the cerebellum's neural activity does not underpin any form of conscious perception and is therefore not part of the NCC. Every subjective, phenomenal state will have an associated NCC. For example, you will have one NCC for seeing the color red, another one for seeing your mother, and a third one for hearing a siren. By deactivating the NCC for any one specific conscious experience, we will affect the perception and cause it to disappear. If the NCC could be artificially induced, perhaps by neurosurgery or cortical microstimulation in a prosthetic device, the person would experience the associated perception. It is important to note that characterizing and discovering the NCC in brains is not the same as developing a theory of consciousness. A theory of consciousness can tell us why particular systems can experience anything, why these systems are conscious, and why other systems are not conscious. Understanding the NCC is, however, a vital step toward developing theories of consciousness.

Consciousness varies in both levels of arousal and content, and there are two types of conscious experiences: *phenomenal*, which occurs in the moment, and *access*, which uses recall of past experiences in order to create consciousness. NCCs are studied by using MRI and EEG scans which locate brain activity and provide visual representations that are precise and measurable. The most widely used stimuli in consciousness research studies are visual stimuli as they are easy to record and manipulate.

Neurophilosophy seems most likely to be able to bridge the gap between the physical and the phenomenal as relates to the consciousness question. The following are some of the questions that neurophilosophy seeks to answer:

- **State Consciousness:** What is the difference between conscious and subconscious mental states?
- **Transitive Consciousness:** What is one conscious of in a mental state that is considered conscious?
- **Phenomenal Character:** When one is in a conscious state, what are the properties to which we make comparison in order to recognize that state?

The question of **state consciousness** focuses on the difference between mental states that are unconscious and mental states that are conscious. In conscious mental states, we have a conscious perception of, for example, the words that you are reading. Our mental states vary, though, in levels of consciousness. Consider, for instance, the memory that you have of your mother's name. Although that memory has been with you for many years, it was not always a conscious memory. At some point between the initial acquisition of the information and the point at which you consciously retrieve it, it was unconscious. This is the question around state consciousness—where or how does that information move between the two states?

The question of **transitive consciousness** addresses the contents of which we are conscious. When we are in a conscious state, we are conscious of a specific thing such as a buzzing insect, for instance. Such things also vary with respect to how conscious we are of them.

Consider a conversation being conducted at a table next to you in a restaurant. You are not actively listening to the conversation, but you are aware of its existence. The question, therefore, is, how is that form of consciousness different from the active form of awareness you have of the conversation at your own table?

The question of **phenomenal character** concerns the properties (also called qualia) of various conscious states. Conscious states have specific properties which make up their phenomenal character. These properties allow us to describe these states as being 'like' something else when we are in that state. When you are consciously aware of a cup of coffee, you would be able to describe it as being like something, otherwise you would not have any perception at all of the cup of coffee. This also raises the question as to whether individual perceptions of the phenomenal character of that cup of coffee may vary from person-to-person. A rather simple example would be that the perception would be based on previous experience with coffee. A person who has enjoyed coffee in the past will have a positive perception of the coffee, and that is how it forms part of their consciousness. A person that is allergic to caffeine will have a completely different perception of the cup of coffee. The question is, does the way we see the coffee change its nature, or is its nature fixed, and only our perception of that nature varies?

Theories around the neurophilosophy of consciousness bring forward the use of neuroscience in answering these three questions of consciousness. It is important for us to understand what motivates the neurophilosophy of consciousness. The predominant answer to that is that neurophilosophy has a certain appeal to those with a leaning toward belief only in the physical, and neurophilosophy is well-suited to bridge the gap between the phenomenal and the physical. By attempting to bridge the gap by reducing phenomenal character down to its chemistry or the microphysics in question, many feel that this is too far a distance to bridge. Perhaps a more plausible ideal is to seek out a higher-level set of physical attributes, such as biological attributes. In considering the available biological phenomena, probably the most plausible attributes are neural in nature.

Neurophilosophist, Paul Churchland, takes what he calls a "dynamic profile approach" to understanding consciousness. This approach sees consciousness as any cognitive representation which is involved in attentive focus which can be shifted onto different aspects of perceptual inputs. It also includes the application of various interpretations of those inputs as well as the holding of the results of interpreted input in short-term memory. According to Churchland's theory, this allows for the representation of temporal sequences.

These four conditions primarily focus on the question, "What makes a state conscious?"

Much of Churchland's discussion of the dynamical profile account of consciousness concerns how the four conditions may be concurrently implemented in ongoing neural networks. Neural networks are groups of connected neurons. These networks have one or more neurons that serve as inputs and also one or more neurons that serve as outputs. In layman's terms, we can consider the input neuron as the receptionist in a company and the output nerve would perhaps be the salesperson who executes the sale after receiving the sales lead from the receptionist. There may also be neurons that are not used for input or output, and these are called interneurons. At any given time, neurons are in one of several states of activation. Input neurons have a state of activation which is caused by receiving a stimulus. Interneurons and output neurons have states of activation which are functions of the states of activation of other neurons that they are connected to. The amount of influence that the activation of one neuron has on another is determined by the strength of the connection between them. The process of learning through neural networks is believed to involve changes in the strength of the connections between neurons. It is also believed to involve the pruning of old connections and the addition of new ones. The brain is regularly performing this activity and neurologists believe that around the age of 16, we have a major 'pruning' of neural networks that have not yet been activated. This is why it is vital to ensure that a child is constantly trying new activities and attempting as many new skills as possible. Interestingly, some mental illnesses including schizophrenia are thought to emanate at this point of major pruning as a result of genetic and environmental factors. This is why most people living with schizophrenia will start to display symptoms in their late teens and early twenties, as the effect of this neural pruning takes hold.

The concept of phenomenal consciousness considers what it means for mental states to be conscious as opposed to the unconscious. It also considers what it means for such states to have phenomenal character, in other words, to have properties in which can be described in terms of: there is "something it's like." Phenomenal consciousness raises many traditional philosophical issues that consider how phenomenal consciousness relates to the rest of the world. Much discussion in philosophical arenas concerns whether the world, as put forward by physical theory, can really accommodate phenomenal consciousness or if we would be left with a dualism that separates reality into a nonphysical phenomenal consciousness and a physical everything else. Even philosophers who agree that phenomenal consciousness is consistent with a belief in physical nature, disagree considerably. One way of viewing this group of issues is to ask which natural science is best suited to study phenomenal consciousness and how the relation between that science should be compared to the sciences that involve the most basic aspects of reality such as the physical sciences. One view is that psychology is the correct science to use for understanding phenomenal consciousness and that any investigation of a psychological nature around phenomenal consciousness should be separate from neuroscience. There is an opposing view that the proper science is neuroscience and contributions from psychology are only theories.

Those who have this view refer to themselves as practitioners of neurophilosophy. Neurophilosophy is a subcategory of naturalized philosophy that embraces the idea that philosophy is continuous with the natural sciences.

Neurophilosophy entered the world of philosophy when Patricia Churchland (wife of Paul Churchland) published her paper, *Neurophilosophy* in 1986. With this publication, Churchland aimed to introduce neuroscience to philosophers and vice versa.

The couple's professional training was primarily philosophical, and their appointments were in departments of philosophy. They would also publish in philosophy journals. Due to this leaning toward philosophy, neuroscience and philosophy don't have equal influence on the concept of neurophilosophy. The primary focus is the development of an academic pursuit for philosophical institutions. Neurophilosophical theories around phenomenal consciousness works to bring neuroscientific theory and data into the realm of philosophical discussion.

With regard to what we are conscious of, Churchland puts forward that a conscious representation could have any subject matter or content. In fact, this approach casts doubt on theories which seek to restrict the content or type of subject matter that is considered as part of consciousness (Mandik, 2017).

Chapter 4:

Psychology of Consciousness—Heal the Mind Through Science

The interest of the psychology community in consciousness is based in methods of healing for the mind. As each of the philosophies we have discussed in prior chapters is considered, the question remains as to how these can be put into practice in order to understand how to correct the course of consciousness when things go wrong. If we gain insight into the nature of consciousness through neurophilosophy, perhaps we can alter states of consciousness in order to also provide healing.

Various forms of psychotherapy, such as cognitive behavioral therapy, rely on understanding how consciousness and its components drive behavior. The act of correcting behavior or shaping new habits is therefore inextricably linked to understand how those actions began to occur in the first place. We cannot only approach this from an emotional standpoint, though, or allocate the existence of negative behaviors to past events, as the brain is far more complex than that.

Consciousness and Psychology

Today, the primary focus of research into consciousness is to understand what it means on a biological and psychological level. Studies often focus on exactly what it means for information to be present in consciousness, and it also seeks to determine the neural and psychological correlates of consciousness. By discovering these correlates, psychology hopes to use this information for therapeutic purposes.

The purpose of studying consciousness as it relates to psychology is to better understand the self and the underlying reasons and factors that cause certain behavior. When these factors are determined, the information can be used to treat behavior and give the person a better understanding of themselves as well as mechanisms through which they can feel better.

Research into consciousness as it relates to psychology has brought forward the clear determination between the subconscious state and the conscious state. Multiple theories have been developed over the years around consciousness and psychology.

These have included the work of **Sigmund Freud** who brought forward theories around the conscious, the preconscious, the unconscious, and how they relate to the id, the ego, and the superego. In Freud's psychoanalytic theory of personality, he states that the conscious mind is made up of everything inside of our awareness. In this context, our awareness is that aspect of our mental processing that we can rationalize and verbalize. As the conscious mind includes such things as perceptions, sensations, feelings, memories, and fantasies, these are the elements of our current awareness. The subconscious, or preconscious, is closely linked to the conscious mind, and it includes things that we are not consciously thinking of at the moment but which we can easily access. Freud believed that things that the conscious mind wants to hide from the spotlight of awareness are pushed into the unconscious mind. Although we are not aware of these thoughts, feelings, emotions, and urges, Freud believed that they would still have an influence on our behavior. He argued that things that are in the unconscious only become available to the conscious mind in disguised forms, such as in dreams. Freud thought that by analyzing the content of our dreams, we would be able to discover those unconscious influences and how they are impacting our conscious actions. Freud often used the iceberg metaphor to explain the two aspects of human personality. He described the tip of the iceberg that can be seen above the water as being representative of the conscious mind. The part of the iceberg beneath the water, which we cannot see, is actually the bulk of the iceberg, and this represents the unconscious. Freud believed that even though the conscious and preconscious are important, they are not nearly as important in explaining human behavior as the unconscious. He believed that the things that are hidden from awareness have the greatest influence on our behaviors and personalities. The term "Freudian slips" originated from Freud's belief that, on occasion, information from our unconscious slips through into our conscious mind.

Perhaps Freud's most influential idea about the human mind, though, was that the psyche has more than one aspect. His personality theory, which was developed in 1923, stated that the psyche is structured into three parts: the id, ego, and superego. All of these develop at different stages in our lives. It is important to clarify that these are systems of thought or consciousness, not structures within the brain. Freud's psychoanalytic theory states that the id is the most instinctual and primitive part of the mind, and it contains aggressive and sexual drives and hidden memories. It contains all the inherited and biological components of the personality which are present at birth. This includes our sexual instinct and aggressive instinct. Both of these are survival instincts, one to procreate and the other to protect ourselves. The id is the impulsive part of our psyche, and it is also unconscious. It immediately responds to basic desires, needs, and urges. The personality of a newborn child consists only of id, and only later do the ego and superego develop. The id remains extremely basic in its function throughout our lives and doesn't evolve or change with experience or over time. This is because the id is not in touch with the outside world at all. The id is not affected by logic or reality, as it operates within the unconscious. The id operates solely on the pleasure principle which denotes that every desire we have must be satisfied immediately, regardless of the consequences of that satisfaction. When the desires of the id are achieved, we experience pleasure, and when its desires are denied we experience tension. The id engages in primitive primary process thinking. Such thinking is irrational, illogical, and fantasy-driven.

The superego is our moral conscience. It incorporates the morals and values of society which we learn from our parents and others. The superego develops when we are between three and five years old during the phallic stage of psychosexual development. The function of the superego is to help control the impulses of the id, especially those which may get us into trouble in society, such as aggression and sex. It also persuades the ego to work toward moral goals rather than only those that are realistic and to strive to achieve perfection. The superego consists of two systems: the ideal self and the conscience. The conscience is able to punish the ego by causing feelings of guilt. If the ego gives in to the demands of the id, the superego may instill feelings of guilt or regret. The ideal self is an imaginary picture of the person we should be and how we should behave. It represents our career aspirations, our treatment of other people, and how we should behave as members of society. The superego constantly weighs our actions and behavior against the ideal self-image and when it finds us to fall short of the ideal, our conscience kicks in and we feel guilt. The superego also controls feelings of pride as a reward when we behave closer to the ideal. If the standard of the ideal self is unrealistically high, then anything the person does will represent failure. The conscience and ideal self are largely determined in childhood and result from parental values and how we were raised.

The ego is part of our mind which represents realism and serves to mediate a happy balance between the desires of the id and the morality of the superego. The ego is modified by the outside world and works by reason. The ego operates according to the reality principle and works out realistic ways of satisfying the demands of the id. This often means that satisfaction is compromised or postponed in order to avoid negative consequences. The ego considers social norms and realities, etiquette, and rules in deciding how best to behave. Like the id, the ego also seeks tension reduction and seeks to avoid pain. Unlike the id, though, the ego is concerned with finding a realistic strategy in order to obtain pleasure. The ego has no concept of morality and something is good simply if it satisfies desires without causing harm to itself or the id. The ego is relatively weak in relation to the id, and the best the ego can do is continue to point the id in the right direction. If the ego fails to use the reality principle and anxiety is experienced, unconscious defense mechanisms are used to ward off unpleasant feelings like anxiety or make good things feel better for the individual. The ego engages in secondary process thinking, which is realistic, rational, and orientated towards problem-solving. If a plan doesn't work, then it is reassessed until a solution is found. This is known as reality testing and enables the person to take control of their impulses and use self-control, through mastery of the ego. An important feature of social and clinical psychology work is to enhance ego functioning and help the client test reality by helping the client to assess their options (McLeod, 2019).

Although each of these has unique features, they all interact to form our overall personality, and neither part should make a greater contribution to an individual's behavior than another. Freud's theories have become a major cornerstone in psychology and psychiatry, and, while some critics feel that his views are too simplistic, many believe that the theories hold water. We know, after all, that a huge amount of our trauma can start in childhood and it would, therefore, make sense if parts of our personality only developed then, wouldn't it? The idea of the "ideal self" is one that will also resonate with many as we are often our own worst critics. If any of these theories are true, these are aspects of ourselves that we will need to work to overcome if we wish to elevate our consciousness.

Developmental Psychology is another arena in which theories of consciousness have been developed, and this area of psychology focuses on how our childhood and adolescence impact the development of our consciousness and psyche. Developmental psychology is a scientific approach that attempts to explain change, growth, and consistency throughout the lifespan. The field looks at how the concepts of feeling, thinking, and behavior change throughout our life. A large portion of theories within the developmental psychology discipline focuses on childhood development, as this is when the most change occurs during our lifespan.

Developmental psychologists study a range of theoretical areas, including social, biological, emotional, and cognitive processes. Empirical data in this field is dominated by psychologists from Western cultures, including Europe and North America, perhaps owing to the cultures around childrearing in those countries. In the 1980s, though, Japanese researchers began making a valid contribution to the field. Three goals of developmental psychology include describing, explaining, and optimizing development. In order to describe development, we need to focus on typical patterns of change (also called normative development) and individual variations in patterns of change (also called idiographic development). Although there are typical pathways of development that most people will tend to follow in their life, there is still significant room for individual differences. Developmental psychologists also seek to explain the changes that have been observed as they relate to normative processes and individual differences. It is often easier to describe the development, though, than to explain precisely how it occurs. Developmental psychologists also seek to discover ways to optimize development and apply their theories to provide practical assistance.

Social Psychology is the third area of psychology in which theories of consciousness are discussed as well the role of our interactions in society and how they play into the development of our consciousness. It is the scientific study of how our thoughts, beliefs, feelings, goals, and intentions are created within a social context and by actual or perceived interactions with others. Social psychology, therefore, looks at human behavior as being influenced by other people and the social context in which this occurs. Social psychologists work with the factors that cause us to behave in a certain way when we are around others, and they also look at the conditions under which some behaviors, actions, and feelings may occur. Some of the topics examined in social psychology include social cognition, the self-concept, social influence, attribution theory, group processes, discrimination, prejudice, aggression, interpersonal processes, stereotypes, and attitudes.

Neuropsychology

Neuropsychology seems to be the branch of psychology that holds the most hope in connecting our consciousness to our behavior. This branch of psychology is concerned with how the brain and the rest of the nervous system influence behavior and cognition. Neuropsychologists often focus on how injury or illness can affect cognitive functions and behaviors. The study of consciousness in neuropsychology has mainly been in relation to attention, perception, language, and memory.

The combination of these themes has seen the emergence of a field called philosophical psychopathology, where mental disorders serve as a springboard for philosophical insight. The field also delves into the connection between damage to the brain and the various states of consciousness.

Neuropsychology deems consciousness to be a global activity of the nervous system. The pathological and physiological aspects of consciousness are usually studied in relation to the Circadian clock, which is our natural sleep-wake cycle, as well as forms of morbid and normal unconsciousness. Neuropsychology has predominantly focused on higher functions such as memory and perception, as well as the disorders that plague these functions. Neuropsychology has been at the forefront of the identification of the conscious and unconscious components of information processing. In a review published in 2019, though, historical steps were presented in the formulation of consciousness as global brain function with its principal ingredients being content and arousal (Berlucchi and Marzi, 2019). The review covers the connection of these functions to the subcortex and the neocortex in the brain. It also shows some new development in cognitive neuroscience and neuropsychology which indicate the importance of the hippocampus in the brain, in thought and dreams. It also indicates that non-neocortical structures in the brain may contribute to the content of consciousness more than was previously thought.

In the past, attempts have been made at finding a location for the emergence of various cognitive functions in the brain. This has predominantly been done by ascertaining which abilities are lost when damage occurs in the brain. Of course, it cannot be assumed that because ability is primarily controlled by a specific part of the brain that there is not a contribution from another area in the brain at some point. Attempts to find a location for the emergence of consciousness have been focused on the causes of unconsciousness, but it is believed that such causal research is misconceived as if consciousness is seen as a global function of the brain, then complete malfunction of consciousness surely cannot be attributed to one incident. Studies have shown that large portions of the brain which are known to be involved in the emergence of consciousness can be removed without causing loss of consciousness. The focusing of consciousness on sleep-wake cycles also seems to be misconceived as being awake does not necessarily mean that one has consciousness, just as being asleep does not imply that one has a lack of consciousness. By the same token, people who are in vegetative states and seemingly unaware of their surroundings are still aware of themselves. The fact that we dream while we are sleeping and that external stimuli can affect the content of our dreams seems to confirm that, even when we are asleep, there is still an element of consciousness.

Although we know that much of the activity that is considered 'intelligent' emanates in the cortex areas of the brain, there is still debate as to whether this is the only area involved in consciousness. There is also an argument around whether consciousness can precede the development of the cortex in fetuses and premature babies as there seem to be appropriate reactions to sensory stimuli along with correlating motor expression. This would imply that consciousness is present despite the cortex not being fully developed or matured.

Consciousness in Therapy

It has been argued that the main use of consciousness in therapy should be to heighten the awareness that the patient has around the behavior they exhibit which may be damaging. By raising awareness of this behavior it is thought the patient can undergo a process of reforming, recognition, and revision. If Freud's theories are to be believed, then we cannot change behaviors without unlocking the unconscious mind. Consider the following two phrases: "I'm of two minds…" and "Part of me agrees with you…" Now consider the reality of what we are saying when we use those phrases. Unless you have multiple personalities, which is highly unlikely, what you are saying is that your consciousness is aware of one option while there is another nagging part of you that is giving you another option but you can't quite put your finger on what or why. Perhaps that "other part" of you is your unconscious. Whether the unconscious is actually a part of our consciousness or not is up for debate, but if information in our unconscious is able to slip through or force itself to be vaguely known to the extent that we know it's there even though we can't completely access it, surely there must be a very close link between the conscious mind and the unconscious mind.

If this link is indeed so close, then perhaps our best option at treating a disturbed or disrupted conscious mind is actually focusing on the unconscious. Later on in this book, we will look at spiritual practices that seek to do exactly that by altering our state of consciousness. How can we use the unconscious in a Western psychotherapy setting, though, in order to impact the consciousness? The first and possibly most important step is to identify whether the behavior is, in fact, being caused by the unconscious or the conscious. While regardless of where the behavior stems from, we still have to take responsibility for it, it may be helpful to acknowledge that if we are struggling to sleep, be creative, or relax, for instance, perhaps we are seeking control in the wrong part of our mind. Often simply by acknowledging that it is not our conscious mind that is directing the behavior, we allow the unconscious mind room to make the required changes and the problem could resolve itself. This is often easier said than done, though, especially if you are a highly analytical person who likes to believe that you are in direct control of everything. Keep in mind, though, that science backs up the existence of a part of our minds which is not lit up by awareness. Different fields may call it different things, but it definitely exists.

We will discuss hypnotherapy in greater detail later but in this context, it is important for us to point out that a trained hypnotherapist is capable of carrying out an act called splitting. By using this technique, they can pick whether they wish to influence the conscious or unconscious mind. This is helpful in trying to deal with behaviors that are rooted in the unconscious mind such as autonomic processes.

Many of the difficulties we encounter with our conscious mind are as a result of it trying to override the unconscious mind and not allowing it to do its work. We can help to avoid this by becoming curious about our consciousness. Give your conscious mind permission to sit back and watch the unconscious mind work. Again, this is a method used in hypnotherapy where the hypnotherapist will speak only to the conscious mind and provide it with the opportunity to "take a break" for a while. One of the easiest ways that we can use this technique ourselves is by framing our thoughts to address that "other hidden part" within us. Use phrases like "I'm addressing the part of myself that knows how to solve this problem. I know that you have the power to help me solve this problem, and I am calling on you to do so now."

A large part of treating our consciousness by using our unconscious mind is developing trust in the latter. You can call your unconscious whatever you like. Labels don't matter. You may have referred to it as your 'gut,' or your "sixth sense" but really, there is nothing mystical about it. It is very simply the part of our consciousness that we are not always aware of. Now think about situations in which you may have made the wrong decision and you've later berated yourself saying, "I should have trusted my gut." What are you actually telling yourself? You are acknowledging that your unconscious mind is far wiser and more knowledgeable than your conscious mind and if you had listened to the instinct that whispered within you, you would have made a better choice. How many times has your "gut instinct" been wrong? The answer is never. There is not one single instant in which your unconscious mind has been wrong if it is presented with all of the required information. This means that if we are able to start training ourselves, and using professionals to help us, to trust our unconscious mind, we are capable of resolving a huge array of behavioral issues within our lives.

As we start to consider how psychology and psychotherapy may just tie in with less 'textbook' ideas such as our unconscious, we must then start to consider that by accessing all parts of our consciousness, we may be capable of astounding things. It is at this point that we should address how altering our state of consciousness may help to access our unconscious mind more easily.

Chapter 5:

Spirituality and Consciousness—The Promise of a Higher Awareness

Although huge progress has been made in the study of consciousness through philosophy and science, many questions remain unanswered. If neither science nor philosophy can answer these questions, then perhaps we should turn to spirituality in our quest to close the gaps. In this chapter, we will approach the unanswered questions of consciousness from a spiritual perspective and seek to investigate the possibility that we could achieve a higher state of consciousness.

The ingratiation of spiritual concepts into the modern, Western world is becoming more common. We have yoga and meditation classes. Science is measuring how these practices actually impact our physical health and, as a result, we find ourselves at the crux of a new dawn in our history. For the first time, the world of spirituality is becoming seamlessly integrated into the world of science. Medically-trained doctors are prescribing practices like fasting, yoga, and mindfulness training as therapeutic methods of improving health. This shift in our society indicates that if we really want to understand the truth behind consciousness, we have no choice but to address the spiritual context as well.

How Spirituality Fits into the Pursuit of Consciousness

Scientific and psychological studies have always approached consciousness with a view to treating mental illness. In quite a parallel view, in the world of spirituality, consciousness takes on quite a different role. In both the East and the West, spiritual approaches define consciousness as a state of awareness of the self and the environment. The ultimate goal of spiritual consciousness, though, is to reach a higher state of awareness, which may be called enlightenment, transcendence, or other oneness, depending on the form of spirituality. In such heightened states of awareness, the spiritualist theory is that we would become god-like, less focused on the self, all-knowing, and completely connected with the universe. It is deemed to be a state of absolute well-being.

The Mayan culture had nine levels of consciousness of which the highest level was the attainment of a god-like state of all-knowing consciousness. This pyramid-like representation of the growth of consciousness works with a timeline and allocates a level of consciousness to each period of time. These levels are not just personal levels through which we as individuals can grow, though; they are actually levels of consciousness which society has reached, and if their pyramid has any basis in fact, we are now in the ninth level. These levels are as follows:

1. **Cellular** (16.4 billion years ago): we developed a reaction/action consciousness. All physical laws were developed as well as chemical compounds. Starfields, solar systems, and planets were developed.
2. **Mammalian** (820 million years ago): we developed stimulus/response consciousness. Individual cells from the previous Cellular cycle started developing survival mechanisms with increased consciousness toward stimuli and responses.
3. **Familial** (41 million years ago): we developed stimulus/individual response consciousness. We began to recognize individuals and the establishment of the family relationship as opposed to herd, school, or flock mentalities.
4. **Tribal** (2 million years ago): we developed similarity/difference consciousness. This period

saw the development of the mind to detect similarities and differences in our experience

5. **Cultural** (102,000 years ago): we developed shared reasoning consciousness. We began to search for reasons for everything, as a basis of all cultural understanding.
6. **National** (3115 BCE): we developed a law consciousness. Our current concept of right and wrong was born.
7. **Planetary** (1755 CE): we developed a power consciousness. Our understanding and drawing of power from natural laws began.
8. **Galactic** (5 January 1999): we developed an ethics consciousness. We began to understand and focus on more advanced ethical matters.
9. **Universal** (10 February 2011): we developed a conscious co-creation form of consciousness. We began to focus on the achievement of godlike status and of an all-knowing consciousness.

One of the criticisms of this system has been that each stage seems to move about 20 times faster than the prior one. If the Mayans are correct, then we are currently experiencing our highest level of consciousness. This pyramid is closely linked to an evolutionary process and it is time-based. This is easy to criticize if we consider that many factors can influence timelines and unless the Mayans were basing the pyramid on precise predictions then it is likely to be inaccurate.

The Inca people had seven levels of consciousness, where the highest level allowed us to unite the child-like parts of ourselves like wonder, creativity, playfulness, spontaneity, and laughter with our adult lives. This state left behind the child-like fears, lack of appreciation for the world's complexity, and naivety, and instead embraced only the positive and useful elements of childhood. Their levels, in contrast to the Mayan levels, were based on a progression of awareness and concern for others. They did not allocate time periods to their consciousness levels and each level consists of an external, visible change, and internal, invisible change. They include:

1. **First:** the external change is our perception of space and time and the internal change is the awareness of the physical body and a focus on individual survival.
2. **Second:** the external change is that good is separated from evil and the internal change is to distinguish the self from others.
3. **Third:** the external change is that we become capable of discrimination and the internal change is that we are capable of choosing to align with goodness rather than evil. This is the level that most people are at.
4. **Fourth:** the external change on this level is that we have reverence for nature, a sense of

oneness, and we are against the harm of others. The internal change is that we have a decreased attachment to material possessions.

5. **Fifth:** the external change here is the ability to heal others in certain circumstances. The internal change is physical, mental, emotional, and spiritual restoration. This level in Incan culture was thought to signal the day of judgment.

6. **Sixth:** the external change here is the ability to heal others in any condition. The internal change is that we no longer have any value in individuality, and we understand the importance of community contribution.

7. **Seventh:** the external change here is that we become the teachers of all others. The internal change exemplifies the principles of honesty, faithfulness, service, and truthfulness.

The Incan levels of consciousness seem more applicable to where we are today as they can be used not just to denote the progress of our consciousness as a society but also as individuals.

Buddhism is thought to offer one of the most complex of all explanations of consciousness among the various spiritual practices. Buddhists acknowledge that the concept of consciousness encompasses a wide range of varied mental activities but they do not attribute these activities to an independent self. Instead, Buddhist theories around the mind focus on the idea that human beings may be reduced to the physical and mental components of which they are made up. Although there is disagreement in modern-day as to the interpretation of the original teachings of Buddha, it is thought that they include the idea that any sensation or consciousness experienced by a human being does not belong to the self and is transitory and simply a result of causally interconnected events. This is referred to as the not-self doctrine.

The not-self doctrine seeks to refute the idea that independence and self-subsistence are valuable ideals and instead promotes the idea that we should not seek to create some sense of identity from the stream of physical and subjective phenomena that we experience. The not-self doctrine describes not only humanity but all the elements that make up our existence as being part of one large entity and not separate or independent. A focus on consciousness itself is not made in many forms of Buddhism, but, where it does appear in teachings, it is painted as a temporary accessing of an overall stream of sensory activity that does not belong to us but is unique in how we access it. Buddhists believe that this ongoing and global mindstream is accessed and then manifested in each being on a moment-by-moment basis. This means that all events, including the formation of consciousness, arise from a series of other causes and conditions to which every being on earth is interconnected.

The Hindu religion uses terms such as higher consciousness, superconsciousness, and God-consciousness to describe the levels of consciousness that can be attained by a human being who has achieved a higher level of awareness. Evolution as described by the Hindu religion is not the biological development human beings have seen as a result of natural selection and genetic advancement but rather the emotional and spiritual advancement that occurs through spiritual practices. The Himalayan Academy lexicon describes consciousness as perception, apprehension, or awareness and states that there are several layers of consciousness from the ordinary consciousness of our body to the omniscient state of superconsciousness. In the Hindu religion, the journey of progressing through various levels of consciousness can be compared to our modern idea of self-improvement.

There are certain parallels in spiritualism to Western philosophies on higher consciousness. One such parallel is the New Age movement which looked forward to a New Age of love and light and provided a foretaste of the coming era through personal transformation and healing. At the center of this movement was the idea of the existence of higher and lower states of consciousness. In this respect, it aligns closely with many Eastern spiritual beliefs that aim to achieve a higher state of consciousness. The strongest supporters of the New Age movement were also followers of modern esotericism, which is a belief system that is based on acquiring mystical knowledge. While academics refer to the system as a religion, followers of the New Age movement reject this and refer to it as spiritualism. Esotericism has been popular in the Western world since the 2nd century. It predicted that a New Age of heightened spiritual consciousness and global peace would arrive and bring an end to poverty, racism, hunger, sickness, and war. The movement incorporated several traditional spiritual practices such as astrology, tarot reading, meditation, and yoga in order to progress through various states of consciousness. An approach that combined Western rationalism and eastern mysticism called Transpersonal psychology encourages the belief that certain consciousness-altering practices can be undertaken separately from the religious or spiritual spheres in which they originated and still provide the same benefits in terms of elevation of consciousness.

There are other models that combine scientific and spiritual approaches to consciousness. One example of this is Leary's 8-Circuit Model of Consciousness. This is a psychologically-based theory that brings together the various interpretations of the main altered states of awareness into a single 'mega-theory.' The theory states that the altered levels of consciousness which are defined in the medical field are products of eight different brain structures within the human nervous system. Critics of Leary's theory argue that the inspiration for it seems to indirectly stem from the Hindu Chakra system. Leary's highest realm of consciousness, called the 8th Psycho-atomic Circuit, allows access to the intergalactic consciousness which is thought to predate life in the universe.

Another example of a combined scientific-spiritual approach to consciousness is Morin's 4-Tiered Integration Model. The highest level of consciousness in this model is called Meta Self-Awareness.

Chapter 6:

Altered States of Consciousness

As we attempt to understand the concept of consciousness, we must also understand and work toward the awareness that consciousness can be altered. Many spiritual practices as well as scientific practices seek to find ways of altering consciousness. In spirituality, this is packaged as finding ways to better understand ourselves and connect with greater consciousness. In the world of science, the altering consciousness comes in the form of psychotherapy.

Many cultures and practices recognize the important influence that consciousness has on the self. An ordinary state of consciousness provides access to an ordinary reality but in altered states of consciousness, such as when we are dreaming, we are permitted contact with non-ordinary reality. Practices that seek to encourage contact with this non-ordinary reality are used for several different purposes such as healing, connecting with the self, connecting with the environment, and connecting with the Divine. All of these are intended to bring one to a higher state of consciousness. Some of the practices which can bring one into a different state of consciousness and awareness include:

- Yoga
- Native American dance
- Voodoo
- Hypnosis
- Holotropic approaches
- Psychedelics

Yoga

Yoga has been practiced for millennia in Asia, and today it is used therapeutically to treat insomnia and a range of psychological problems. The intention of practicing yoga is to gain awareness of the physical sensations and perceptions, while retaining a non-judgmental view of these sensations. It is also important to ensure that the ego does not play a role in any thoughts or feelings experienced while practicing yoga. In order to attain this state, visualization techniques are used in combination with specific physical postures and controlled breathing. Interestingly, the state which is attained while practicing yoga is similar in a neurophysiological sense to those who smoke opium. This has led to a hypothesis that endorphins are released during the practice which accounts for these feelings.

Practitioners believe that yoga helps us connect with our true nature and the nature of the universe itself in a way that may be as valuable as the discoveries of modern science. The practice of yoga is defined as a *vidya* or a way of knowledge. Yoga, which means *union*, aims at reuniting the individual human being with the universal and transcendent consciousness. This requires a radical change in how we feel, think, and look at life. Yoga in its original sense is a science of consciousness and was used to show those practicing it how to develop higher awareness. Practitioners admit that this is not to say that yoga is the same as science but rather that it constitutes a different type of science with its own methodology and value that can complement what science offers.

As a term, yoga arose in Vedic texts, which started with the mantras of the Rigveda, one of the oldest books in the world. Yoga as a practice or philosophy was first articulated in the *Upanishads* that discuss the nature of consciousness according to an inquiry into the most fundamental question of human life, "Who am I?" Upanishadic teachings are summarized in the *Bhagavad Gita*, which teaches various aspects of yoga. The primary principles of yoga were developed in a brief form in the *Yoga Sutras*. Many different Yoga teachings eventually arose and expanded into a larger system with many facets.

The *Yoga Sutras* define yoga as *citta vritti nirodha*, or "calming the movements of the mind," which is our conditioned or individual form of consciousness. This definition implies an observation and analysis of all our mental activities. These are described as wrong knowledge, memory, right knowledge, imagination, and sleep. Yoga consists not merely of an intellectual examination but a profound meditative inquiry. Yoga correlates with *samadhi*, which is the ultimate stage of yoga practice. *Samadhi* is the state of unity consciousness in which the agitation of the mind is put to rest, and, instead, it comes to act as a mirror, reflecting the truth of reality.

Today, yoga has become very popular as a form of exercise and it is revered for its relaxation and physical health benefits. Yoga can be practiced in classes or as individuals once you learn the basic poses and breathing.

Native American Dance

Many of the native American people have long practiced healing dances in which a person is brought into an altered state of consciousness by an initiator and aided by the community. There is usually no use of hallucinogens in these dances, but, instead, the altered states are brought about by shifting the sleep-wake cycle, hyperventilation and hypoventilation, and rhythmic stimulation of the sense of hearing and motor functions. If we look at Native American dance from a Western psychotherapy perspective, we can relate to several of the practices as being similar to group psychotherapy, activation, and occupational therapy, the process of reliving a trauma (which is referred to as cathartic abreaction), psychodrama, and physical exercise. There is an additional psychosocial function to these dances, especially when they are conducted today, in that they provide a cultural bond to a people who have had their cultural practices eroded by modern society.

Although Native American people, like many other indigenous peoples worldwide, speak of various concepts which are abstract to non-native people, consciousness is not spoken of in an explicit sense. By learning the teachings of native people about cosmology, the Good Medicine Path, and healing, though, we see that there is actually a consistent practical view of consciousness that exists throughout all of their teachings. Such knowledge is passed down through generations of Native American people with the understanding that once they have received those teachings, they are also given the responsibility to live their lives accordingly. When we focus on searching for discussions around consciousness in the teachings of native people, it becomes all the more apparent that the very concept is transient and changes depending on the culture in question. Perhaps the reason that consciousness is not explicitly spoken about in Native American culture is that all of their teachings, practices, and their very way of life are aimed at elevating states of consciousness.

Voodoo

Haitian healing ceremonies through the practice of voodoo use psychophysical techniques to manipulate consciousness. Followers use these ceremonies to rectify disorders which they believe to be caused by ethical or religious errors, and spiritual, magic, or karmic forces. Therapeutic ceremonies are conducted by mediums and the person is placed into an altered state of consciousness under the influence of the spirit of a deceased person. From a Western perspective, this altered state seems to be brought on by an overload of the senses with sights and sounds being presented in a rhythmic manner.

Hypnosis

This practice is used frequently in the Western world in psychotherapy to help heal traumas and other applications, and it is also used in victims or witnesses of crime to help retrieve information that is 'locked' in the subconscious. The hypnotic state is best defined as an altered state of consciousness in which receptiveness and attention is heightened and the awareness of the periphery is temporarily suspended.

Some experts believe that the hypnotic state does not, in fact, exist and what is witnessed, instead, is a reaction from the individual to the societal role they are expected to play as the patient and the authoritarian role played by the hypnotist. The susceptibility to being hypnotized varies widely from person-to-person and also throughout a specific person's lifetime. It is widely believed that susceptibility to hypnosis could relate to the rapport that the hypnotist is able to establish with the person they are attempting to hypnotize. In order to induce hypnosis, the subject is usually placed in an area where there is little to no visual or auditory stimuli, therefore, making it easier for the person to focus solely on the voice of the hypnotist. Hypnosis is an altered state of consciousness that is very similar to others we encounter in daily life such as deep concentration and relaxation. It is not a sleep state, which is a common misconception, and there is significant neurological evidence to prove that brain activity during sleep is very different from brain activity during hypnosis.

Holotropic Approaches

This method of therapy facilitates altered states of consciousness by using evocative music, focused bodywork, and conscious breathing. This approach is used to bring elements of the subconscious into the conscious realm. As many psychological issues have their roots in childhood, and much of this trauma may be locked in the subconscious, physical or mental symptoms of this trauma is seen as the first level of healing. Patients are then guided to resolve the trauma through various levels of holotropic therapy.

Also called holotropic breathwork, the approach has become increasingly popular among those seeking to explore an alternate process of self-healing to attain a state of wholeness. This unconventional New Age practice was developed in the 1970s by psychiatrists Stanislav and Christina Grof in order to achieve altered states of consciousness, without the use of drugs, as a potential therapeutic tool. It involves quickening and controlling breathing patterns in order to influence your emotional, mental, and physical states. As a practice, it is derived from a spiritual framework, but is also a trademarked activity. In many countries, practitioners use the technique as a spiritual practice rather than a therapeutic one, and some people participate to expand their awareness rather than to overcome or manage a mental health condition. Many proponents of holotropic breathwork believe that this technique moves you toward a higher state of consciousness. It is believed to shift you into another state, which can be appealing if you feel stagnant and unable to advance. Often, this feeling of awakening occurs through some form of catharsis. It is believed, though, that trauma will only come forward during a holotropic breathwork session if it is necessary for healing, and that this will be unknown at the outset of the session. Each person's experience with the practice is self-directed and unique, unfolding on its own as the practice progresses.

Psychedelics

Psychedelics, which are often referred to as hallucinogens, are psychoactive substances that produce changes in mood, perception, and the cognitive process. Psychedelics affect all of the senses and alter our sense of time, our thinking, and our emotions. There has been much debate in academic and popular literature around the issue of psychedelics actually allowing us to enter a higher state of consciousness. There are differences in the states that various psychedelics produce and these effects also differ between individuals. One of the major associations made with the use of psychedelics is that they are 'mind-expanding.' From a scientific or psychological viewpoint, this mind expansion may mean that the drugs are allowing content that would usually not form part of our consciousness to enter our minds. This content may ordinarily form part of the subconscious of which we are not aware at all times and in ordinary states. The predominant change seen in psychedelic states is an increase and shift in visual imagery, including reports of many different colors being visible as well as the witnessing of scenes either from the past or scenes with which they are not familiar but seem other-worldly. There is certainly compelling evidence that the use of psychedelics increases the amount of sensory information that is received at any given time. Some users of psychedelics have reported difficulty in decision-making, perhaps as a result of this overwhelming amount of sensory information being received. Many users, however, report an increase in creativity and other aspects of cognitive functioning (Bayne and Carter, 2018.)

In the 1950s, several groups of psychiatrists carried out a series of studies into the therapeutic potential of psychedelic drugs. Their work produced preliminary evidence that LSD may be effective in treating various psychiatric conditions as well as alcoholism. When the substance was made illegal during the War Against Drugs, though, research was halted. The psychedelic research moratorium would go on to last nearly thirty years. In the 1990s, researchers began to indicate a renewed interest in the therapeutic potential of psychedelics, and today there are dedicated research teams based around the world. In April 2019, the world's first Center for Psychedelic Research was launched at the Imperial College in London, and in September of the same year, Johns Hopkins University launched its own center for Psychedelic and Consciousness Research. Scientists are now studying how psychedelics affect the brain. These studies include human clinical trials to test their efficacy in treating drug-resistant depression and post-traumatic stress disorder. The director of the Center for Psychedelic Research at Imperial College, Robin Carhart-Harris, and his colleague Gregory Scott, have proposed the use of psilocybin, which is the psychoactive ingredient in magic mushrooms, as a treatment for disorders of consciousness. This proposal has raised several ethical questions.

Disorders of consciousness typically occur following severe brain injury when the brain systems controlling arousal and conscious awareness are disrupted. An example of this may be a coma patient that shows no signs of conscious awareness or being awake. A standard comatose state post brain injury usually lasts up to one month. After that, a patient will usually either progress into a vegetative state, in which they are awake but show no signs of awareness, or into a minimally-conscious state. Interestingly, patients are more likely to recover from the minimally-conscious state than from the vegetative state. Currently, though, it is very difficult for doctors to tell these two states apart as levels of awareness differ so greatly. The proposal to use psychedelics as a treatment for patients with consciousness disorders is born from a theoretical concept regarding brain complexity. As we have learned, the brain of a vertebrate is split into localized areas that differ in their function and structure, but behavior and perception require a global integration of information across all of these areas. The complexity of the brain is essentially a measure of the interplay between integration and segregation. Some researchers have linked measures of conscious awareness to levels of brain complexity, and they believe that complexity should be at high levels during the normal waking state and reduced in states where consciousness is lost. Some of these assumptions have been proven in experiments, and there is also some evidence that psychedelic drugs increase brain complexity in humans. From this follows the belief that psychedelics might increase brain complexity in patients with consciousness disorders, leading to heightened levels of conscious awareness. These studies have been slow in taking off as the question of consent has been raised since a patient cannot agree to take a drug when they are not conscious and the application of the drug would not fall within the standard realm of care.

Choosing a Method of Altering Consciousness

There is clearly a wide variety of ways that have been developed throughout our history as humans, as well as methods that are still being developed, in an attempt to alter our state of consciousness. Each individual will get different results from different methods and more important than the level of result is safety. On your journey to increasing and altering your state of consciousness, always ensure that you are approaching methods with the greatest of care. Research any method that you wish to try exhaustively, speak to experts, and ask as many questions as you can. Your belief system and lifestyle will likely dictate which method you try, if any. Starting with the more easily accessible methods such as yoga, meditation, or mindfulness practice is a good idea. As you start to see results, you will be able to build on them. Any attempt to increase your level of consciousness is already a step in the right direction.

Although we have covered the popular methods of altering our state of consciousness here, there are many other cultural and spiritual methods. The most important factor when choosing a method to try is that it does not have any harmful long-term effects. Altering your state of consciousness should always be a positive experience but be warned that if you are harboring deep-seated trauma, it is possible for this to be uprooted from your subconscious when you alter your state of consciousness. This is not necessarily a bad thing, as it gives you the opportunity to deal with it and start healing, but it is recommended that you always ensure that you are safe and protected both emotionally and physically at all times.

Chapter 7:

A Simple Guide to a Higher State of Consciousness

We have explored the concept of consciousness as well as the various approaches to the concept from schools of thought including spirituality, religion, philosophy, and psychology. In this chapter, we will offer some key ideas which are an amalgamation of many of these approaches. These ideas will help to increase one's state of consciousness even if you do not subscribe to a particular form of spirituality or religion.

All of the theories and practices that we have discussed thus far are intended to create an understanding of the evolution of thought and practices on consciousness throughout the ages. In previous chapters, we have approached the larger questions about what consciousness is, how science seeks to use it to treat mental illness, and how it is used in spirituality to achieve a higher state of awareness. All of this information deals with how understanding consciousness can potentially lead to a better and healthier state of being. Finding a method of increasing levels of consciousness is a very individual journey and only you can choose which methods will best be suited to you. The ideas that we have assembled here deal with a combination of ideas from various philosophies, psychological approaches, and spiritual concepts, which are believed to help us achieve a higher state of consciousness.

Many of these ideas may seem very simple and not 'groundbreaking' but they are likely things that you are not focusing on at present. In the journey to a state of higher consciousness, each small step can have a major impact. We recommend that you try some of the following suggestions.

Simple Steps to Achieving Higher Consciousness

1. **Practice mindfulness.** Keep your attention grounded on what is happening in the present moment and how your consciousness is impacted by your senses.
2. **Always work toward completing tasks.** Unfinished tasks cloud our consciousness even if we are not aware of them. This clouding causes our energy to become stagnant and unfocused. By completing even the smallest of tasks, we allow our consciousness to close the door on that thought process.

3. **Focus on doing things to the best of your ability.** By focusing on doing every task that you carry out as well as you can, you do not carry around regret in your consciousness.
4. **Be aware of what you are attached to or what you are developing attachments to.** This includes people, activities, and objects. Although something may seem enjoyable at the time, if it proves to be a negative force in your life in the long-term, it is preferable to remove it from your life early on.
5. **Be generous but without doing so publicly.** Although it may feel good to be acknowledged and rewarded for your generosity, such acts do not help to lift you to a higher state of consciousness. Instead, keep your acts of generosity and philanthropy private.
6. **Treat strangers as you would family members.** In a higher state of consciousness, there is no individual, there is only the concept of living beings. You have come to be in your genetic family quite by chance, so there seems little reason that we should treat strangers any differently than we would our family. If we can overcome the idea of 'them' and 'us' in all respects and instead focus on the unity of beings, we are taking a great step toward higher consciousness.

7. **Create organization from disorganization.** Everything in the universe has its place, and, as such, when we create disorganization in our lives in any sense, we encourage a disturbance of our consciousness.
8. **Practice gratitude.** This does not just apply to gifts in our life that we may immediately see as blessings but also the small blessings that are present even in the most difficult of situations. It is not enough to simply say that you are grateful. In order for your gratitude to increase your level of consciousness, it must be practiced and consciously embraced.
9. **Refuse to place labels upon yourself.** When we attempt to define ourselves as beings, we encourage limitations as all definitions have boundaries and end-points. By encouraging self-limiting beliefs through the use of labels, we suppress our consciousness. Removing labels from your picture of yourself can be a difficult process as we are given labels by society throughout our lives.
10. **Don't steal or lie.** By stealing or lying we don't hurt others as much as we hurt ourselves, because although we may tell ourselves it doesn't matter, it does matter in terms of our consciousness and those acts will always remain on your psyche.

11. **Help others but don't carry them.** It is important for us to live a life of service to others and help wherever we can, but we should not help so much as to make another person dependent on us, as then we are not really doing them a service at all.
12. **Do not encourage others to model your behavior.** Although we are all of one consciousness, each of us is still on our own unique journey, and there is no reason for us to attempt to force another's path in the same direction as ours. We can share our wisdom and hope that the other will find their own path through that wisdom, but we should never encourage another to be just like us.
13. **Set goals and accomplish them.** Often by setting goals for ourselves that involve our day-to-day lives, we can encourage progress in our consciousness. The motivation, courage, and persistence that it takes to accomplish goals that you have set for yourself in your career are skills that will aid you in your personal growth journey as well.
14. **Be careful about how much space you take up.** Of course, this is not related to physical space but rather universal space. Although you are an independent being who is entitled to having your own needs met, this doesn't mean

that you are the only one who deserves that. This universe must serve us all and if we take more than our fair share, we will most certainly not achieve a higher state of consciousness.

15. **Move and speak purposefully.** We often waste so much of our energy jabbering away to fill the void or rushing about without purpose, and that all detracts from the energy we could be using to increase our levels of consciousness.

16. **Do not be impressed by strong personalities.** It is easy to be loud, aggressive, and take up a lot of space in a room; there is nothing impressive about that. What is impressive is having the level of awareness to find strength in your silence. Do not allow yourself to be in awe of a person's arrogance, as that does not improve your level of consciousness.

17. **No person or object is your possession.** Consider people and objects to be moving through your life for only a short space of time. Ownership is not a concept that moves you to a higher plane of consciousness. We are all part of one consciousness, and, as such, it is not possible for one person to have possession of another or even for us to have possession of objects.

18. **Remember to share.** Just as we belong to a single large consciousness which we share with others, it is important for us to share all of our skills, talents, and the objects that currently occupy our physical space with others. The more we give away, the more we are capable of receiving.
19. **Do not seduce.** This does not have to be simply from a sexual perspective. It essentially means that by convincing someone to do your bidding when that was not their original intention, you are taking away their right to choose and detracting from the positive energy in your life. Surely, you want people to be in your life because they have chosen to be there?
20. **Do not overeat or oversleep.** This fits in well with the concept of only taking what we need from the universe so that there will be sufficient resources for everyone.
21. **Do not speak excessively about your personal problems.** Sometimes we just need to share and that's okay, but when we consistently speak our problems into existence we only reinforce their strength in our lives. Share with a person you trust, if you need to, and then move on.

22. **Do not be critical or judgmental if you have little knowledge of the situation.** This certainly applies to our modern world in which we feel quite justified to judge and criticize people we haven't even met on social media and the like. This certainly does not improve our level of consciousness. It also does not help us to be more empathetic.
23. **Choose your friendships wisely.** You will become much like the people with whom you choose to spend your time, so choose people who will help you to increase your level of consciousness and not pull you down.
24. **Don't be a slave to fashion.** If something resonates with you, enjoy it, but don't take part in something because it resonates with others. That is their journey, not yours.
25. **Respect contracts that you have signed.** This goes for verbal and written contracts and, really, any point at which you have given your word to do something. Even though we can pretend that we don't care in our thoughts, our consciousness becomes muddied by every broken promise.
26. **Don't be late.** Considering how limited our time on earth appears to be, it is vital that we do not condone the wasting of it. Being on time for appointments, meetings, and dates,

regardless of whom they are with, is a reflection of your respect for the limited time of another being.

27. **Do not entertain envy.** If we hope to live in a higher state of consciousness, it is imperative that we do not seek to live the lives of others. The previous discussion about disowning the concept of possession applies here as well. If no one truly owns anything, then why should anyone be envious of another?

28. **Don't focus on the monetary profit that your work will bring but rather how it will add back into the greater good.** Financial gain is fleeting; it comes in and it goes out and it's gone. To have changed something permanently for the better, though, allows us to enjoy our achievement forever and that positive energy increases our level of consciousness.

29. **Always put yourself in the other person's shoes.** Most disagreements would be easily resolved if we could just take a moment to try and understand how the other person feels and where they are coming from. Before you start an argument or voice a disagreement ask yourself, "How would I feel if…"

30. **Don't ignore your fears, work toward conquering them.** Our fears may actually represent our desires, and if we work toward

conquering them, we invite our greatest desires into our lives.

31. **Do not react to praise or blame.** One of the most important aspects of gaining a higher consciousness is to reject the necessity for external approval. If we are living to our purpose, that should be the only approval we need.
32. **Work toward creating dignity from pride.** Pride when held too closely almost never has an elevating outcome. Dignity, on the other hand, is a quality in line with higher consciousness.
33. **Do not allow your self-talk to involve either praise or insult.** While it is important for us to push ourselves to be better and allow ourselves to feel elevated when we achieve success, by excessively praising or criticizing yourself, you only run the risk of keeping yourself at a lower plane of consciousness.
34. **Do not abuse your power.** If you are in a position of leadership, do not allow yourself to become abusive or self-serving. Instead, see it as an opportunity to serve others.
35. **Embrace your imagination.** In order to live on a higher level of consciousness, it is vital that we stop only embracing what we can see with our five senses but also that which we can imagine existing.

36. **Don't make others feel admiration, pity, complicity, or sympathy for you.** These are not qualities that increase our level of consciousness; in fact, they only degrade it.
37. **Don't value yourself by your appearance.** While we should certainly do our best to care for the vessel that carries our consciousness, there is no value attached to that vessel. Your consciousness is not dependent on the appearance of your body and, therefore, in this journey to higher consciousness, your body should play no role.
38. **Do not seek out debt or allow it to become stagnant.** Financial and emotional debts will weigh upon your consciousness, taking up space that could be used for positive energy. If you have acquired any form of debt, start working to settle it immediately.
39. **If you offend someone, seek their forgiveness.** Requesting forgiveness does not mean that it will be given but the act of seeking it is your redemption and elevates your consciousness. The person who you have wronged or offended is still on their own path and may, or may not, be in a place to forgive you. That is not your business. If you have wronged someone publicly, don't seek their

forgiveness in private. A wrong must be righted in the realm in which it was created.

40. **Do not keep objects that are useless to you.** Live a minimalist lifestyle and keep only that which brings you joy or has a purpose. Allowing inanimate objects to clutter up your environment also clutters up your consciousness.

41. **Embrace truth.** Falsehoods, lies, and deceit of any kind lower your level of consciousness. Fear of accepting the truth is also a burden on consciousness. Take the opportunity to take a long and deep look at each aspect of your life including your relationships, career, and who you are as a person. Face the things that you have been hiding from. Lying to yourself is sometimes more damaging than lying to others. Recognize that there will be consequences from living in truth because not everyone is prepared to experience the truth, but it is vital to elevating your consciousness.

42. **Be courageous.** Cowardice lowers your consciousness. Courage is the gap between unconscious and conscious growth. If you constantly allow yourself to live in fear, you will find that the universe continually places problems in your way in order to make you face that fear. When you embrace and work on your

courage and face the things that are plaguing you, you will start to grow in your consciousness.

43. **Be compassionate.** Cruelty of any form has no place in the life of a person on a higher level of consciousness. Actively seek out instances in your life where you are displaying cruelty. This takes a lot of courage as often we don't want to admit our own cruelty. To be compassionate means that we need to feel connected to everything that exists. The greater this connection becomes, the more aware you will be of your link to other beings.

44. **Reject apathy.** Raising your consciousness does not mean that you bumble through life accepting whatever comes your way. Quite the opposite is true. When you have a very clear focus in life, all of the energies in the universe will come together to help you achieve that goal. Achieve clarity in your mind and you will have the power to think and act in an intelligent manner. Being unclear about your desires muddies your consciousness as your focus is all over the place and you simply remain in one place.

45. **Practice focusing your attention.** Meditation and the practice of mindfulness is a great way to achieve this. Throughout your day, focus only

on what is before you at that moment. If distracting thoughts enter your mind, acknowledge them and ask them to move on until it is their time to be focused upon.

46. **Work toward gaining knowledge.** You cannot exist on a higher plane of consciousness if you are ignorant. Do not walk through your day with blinkers on. See yourself as a sponge as you go through life and soak up every bit of knowledge available to you.

47. **Be logical.** Irrationality lowers your level of consciousness and logic can be a powerful tool of consciousness. Train yourself to apply critical, logical thinking in all situations, especially when emotions are high and you are most likely to become irrational.

48. **Seek out conscious people.** Focus on spending more time with people who are already at a higher level of consciousness as they will encourage your thinking to their level. Do not completely avoid those who are at a lower level of consciousness, though, because they will help to learn and identify the areas in which consciousness can be improved.

49. **Embrace energy.** Care for and guard your physical and emotional energy. Find ways to increase it and avoid situations that deplete your energy. Physical energy is vital to our

interactions with the world and therefore to increase our consciousness. Care for your body and its energy by exercising and being deliberate and aware of what you are putting into your body.

50. **Address your intention.** We all have freedom of choice and, as human beings, it is common for us to choose actions and habits that are self-destructive. There is no magic tonic to increasing your consciousness. It is a choice that you make, or don't make, every minute of every day. Solidify your intention in your mind so that all of the energies that make up your body and your being are aligned to that intention.

51. **If you do not have faith in yourself or a situation, pretend that you do.** Being uncertain is not uncommon, but it does detract from our ability to elevate our consciousness. The best state for elevated consciousness is one where we are decisive and purposeful.

52. **Do not waste your time trying to eliminate things.** Energy cannot be destroyed. We know this even in the scientific realm; therefore, instead of attempting to eliminate any form of negative energy, work on transforming it into something positive and beneficial to you.

53. **Do not attempt to get services for free.** Everyone's time is valuable, and no one should be taken advantage of.
54. **Do not defend extinct ideas simply because you were the one that voiced them.** Be open to change and improvement. Don't allow yourself to hang on to an idea or belief because it would be embarrassing for you to admit that you were once wrong.
55. **Do not speak of yourself as an unchangeable thing.** When we label ourselves, we forget that we are always capable of growth and improvement.

Only when we make an intentional effort to slow down can we achieve higher levels of consciousness. As you raise your consciousness, you awaken to the eternal, unlimited nature of your being. Higher consciousness is an ever-increasing awareness of the meaning of existence, your spiritual essence, and of the spiritual or energetic nature in all things. Heightened consciousness is something that surpasses our ordinary, conscious mind.

We tend to believe that we are separate from everything else and that we are alone and vulnerable. When we allow this belief to overwhelm us, we get stuck in low consciousness because we are convinced that we are disconnected, alone, and separate. If a feeling of separateness is holding you back from increasing your level of consciousness, consider a droplet of water. When it is on its own, it appears to have a beginning and an end, but if you focus on it, you will see that it is constantly working its way toward joining a larger body of water. When it does, you can no longer see its limitations. Higher consciousness is our larger body of water. Our universal energy field has no surface and no boundaries, and, as such, we can never be separate from it. Each and every one of us is an ocean of conscious energy. At the higher levels of consciousness, we no longer feel separate. We feel, know, and experience oneness with the universal energy field. We are points of energy, but energy has no limits, only characteristics.

Through meditation and other spiritual practices, including mindfulness practice, the development of intuition, and the teachings of the ancient spiritual masters, you can elevate your consciousness to a higher level. Which of these practices you choose is completely up to you.

The beauty of elevating your consciousness is that you are not changing into anything, you are simply becoming a better and improved version of yourself. When we research various spiritual practices, we may become aware that we are operating as only partially conscious beings as our minds are untrained, and we are preoccupied with more base desires. Most human beings are in a state of sleep even when we are awake, as we are blind to the true nature of our existence. We see what we believe is reality, but what we are actually perceiving is seen through the unconscious lenses of our past conditioning, which is completely different from that of any other human being. Therefore, each and every single person alive today lives a slightly different reality and owns a different truth. On a deeper level, this means that each of us creates our own version of reality and our own universe. The possibilities are endless. The beginning of your awakening to higher consciousness is to accept that you are not separate from anyone else.

By practicing mastery of your thoughts and emotion, and embracing and embodying the concepts of understanding, compassion, gratitude, forgiveness, unconditional love, kindness, patience, truthfulness, and humility, you will reach a higher level of consciousness.

At the exceptionally high levels of consciousness, you don't master your thoughts anymore; instead, you transcend them. You become intensely aware of the true nature of reality, without the constant mental chatter and critique of seeking definitions. This level of self-control is difficult but not impossible to achieve. Anyone who is serious about transcending the mind and elevating themselves to that higher level of consciousness can do so.

The mind is difficult to master, and it must therefore be done in small, incremental steps. You have to learn to master your emotions, thoughts, body, mind's wandering, and your habit of living in the past and the future rather than the present. When you are finally able to see reality as it is without the lenses of your conditioning, and when you are able to raise your energetic vibration through the use of the correct thoughts, words, and actions, then you will continue to elevate yourself to higher consciousness. You can alter your state of consciousness anytime when you meditate, engage in yoga or other spiritual practices, or engage in activities that induce an altered state.

These states are a preview of an equally real, parallel world that you create. One way to begin your journey to higher consciousness right now is to say, think, and do things that only feel good and right and avoid things that feel wrong. By doing this, you will begin vibrating at a higher level, and that process will start the instant you make those choices; you will also begin to attract correspondingly high-vibrating energies.

Just a glimpse of your true nature is compelling enough to want to take on this journey.

Christian monks, Hindu sages, and Buddhist ascetics all speak of reaching moments of "higher consciousness," through chanting, meditation, fasting, or pilgrimages. The good news that no matter who you are or what your beliefs are, this state of higher consciousness is possible for you. While it is interesting to learn about some of the ways that others have managed to achieve higher consciousness, only by beginning your own journey will you find the right way for you. As human beings, we spend a lot of our lives in states of lower consciousness, where what we are principally concerned with is ourselves, our survival, and our own success. Ordinary life rewards practical, self-justifying outlooks, and not introspective views that are actually the hallmarks of lower consciousness. When neuroscientists speak of a lower part of the brain, they refer to the reptilian mind and explain that when we are controlled by this part of our brain, we blame others, strike back when we're hit, push away questions that lack immediate relevance, fail to freely associate concepts, and stick closely to a flattering image of where we are heading and who we are. In rare moments, though, when there are no demands or threats against us, late at night or early in the morning, and when our bodies and desires are comfortable and met, we access a privileged part of the higher mind, the neocortex and the seat of empathy, imagination, and impartial judgment. We loosen our grasp on our own ego and rise to a less-biased, more universal perspective, casting away some of the customary 'normal' anxious self-justification and fragile pride. When we are in such states, our mind moves beyond its particular cravings and self-interests. We start to think of other people in a way that is more imaginative. Rather than being critical and aggressive, we are free to consider that their behavior is driven by pressures from their own reptilian brains, which they generally cannot tell us about. We see that their viciousness or temper are actually symptoms of pain and trauma rather than of intentional evil.

It is an astonishing and gradual evolution to allow ourselves to explain the actions of others in terms of their distress, rather than simply how it affects us. In this state, we perceive that the appropriate response to humanity is not fear, cynicism, or aggression but always love. At such moments, the world seems to be quite a different place. It seems to be one of suffering and misguided effort, filled with people that are striving to be heard and, as a result, lashing out. We also see it as a place of beauty, tenderness, longing, and touching vulnerability. The only fitting response, it seems, is universal empathy and kindness. One's own life feels less precious, and one can actually contemplate no longer being present with tranquility. Our own interests are put aside and we may be able to imaginatively fuse with transient or natural things like trees, clouds, waves, the wind, or a moth fluttering around a light. From this point of view, possessions don't matter, status is nothing, and grievances lose their seeming importance. If other people encountered us at this moment, they may be amazed at our transformation and at our newfound empathy and generosity.

States of higher consciousness are often short-lived though. We should certainly make the most of them when they arise and make use of their insights for the time when we need them most. Higher consciousness is a huge win over the primitive mindset which cannot see any such possibilities.

One of the best ways to work toward higher consciousness and also one of the most simple is working on reducing our reactivity. Resolving reactivity quickly and easily reveals higher states of consciousness. Psychiatrist Roberto Assagioli says "On a low level of consciousness there are no solutions, and on a high level of consciousness there are no problems." When we are in some pain whether emotional or physical, the tension puts us into a reactive state. Reactive states feel lower than more expanded states as they feel contracted. We often don't want to consider why we are behaving or feeling the way that we are, we just want to know how to fix it, but there is very little possibility for the elevation of consciousness in immediately feeling better. It is, after all, the journey to the goal that enlightens us and not simply reaching it.

Another pretty simple way to start living on a higher level of consciousness right now is to stop thinking so much. Thinking engages our conscious mind and does not give our unconscious mind the opportunity to take over. You can't unlock higher levels of consciousness if you're always thinking. This is a problem for most people and if you think about it, it is probably a problem for you too.

When you think too much, you overthink. Overthinking blocks your mind from going anywhere beyond itself. You overthink when your life is out of balance. Try practicing clearing up the chaos in your life by taking a break from the thinking that caused it in the first place. If you are going to think, change what you are thinking about. Instead of thinking about your problems, challenges, and other limiting thoughts, spend time thinking about how humans are connected and how powerful the concept of love is. Think about how it is possible that you may be connected to a plant or a bird, or even to a person that you don't like very much.

Most importantly, make continuous efforts to be better than you were the day before. Some days you will succeed and other days you will be less successful, but as long as you are making an effort every day, you are moving forward in your journey.

Chapter 8:

The Bigger Question: Consciousness and the Dilemma of Choice

When we seek to expand and elevate our consciousness, we also find ourselves in a dilemma as we are suddenly responsible for our own actions, thoughts, and beings. Morality is a concept that comes up quite frequently in the discussion of consciousness. What does it mean to be moral and how does it tie into consciousness? In this chapter, we will explore the question of responsibility and morality that emanates when we begin to expand our consciousness.

Quite plainly, there is no such thing as morality if we are not conscious of our behavior and actions. An animal, for instance, cannot be held responsible for its actions because it operates at a lower level of consciousness than human beings are able to attain. We cannot say an animal's actions are moral or immoral, they simply behave as animals instinctively behave. This is, therefore, the difference between the ability to increase our level of consciousness or simply continuing through life at a base level of survival. This is the dilemma of increasing our level of consciousness. We cannot be responsible for things we are not aware of, but when we seek to purposefully increase that level of awareness, our responsibility for our actions increases in equal measures.

For example, if you are not aware of the issue of global warming then you cannot be held responsible for contributing towards it. When you are made aware of the issue, though, you automatically take on personal responsibility for not contributing to the problem. By the same token, if you are aware that you are feeling anxious, then the responsibility for quelling that anxiety becomes your own. When you are made aware that you are hurting someone, you are responsible for changing your behavior in order to stop hurting them.

In the book, *Consciousness and Moral Responsibility*, author Neil Levy presents his ideas around what he calls the *consciousness thesis*. Levy maintains that awareness of the facts that provide moral significance to our actions is necessary in order for us to be morally responsible. As consciousness is the key to integrating the representations that we have of the world around us if our behavior is driven by unconscious representations (that of which we do not have awareness) then that behavior will be stereotyped and inflexible. We can only interact fully with a representation when it becomes conscious and, indeed, it is at this point that we develop responsibility for molding our behavior to match our new awareness. Perhaps the most succinct layman's expression of this notion is, "When we know better, we do better." In fact, though, from a perspective of consciousness we should say, "When we know better, we have the responsibility to do better."

In the final section of *Consciousness and Moral Responsibility*, Levy addresses the concerns of theorists who worry that the ever-present nature and power of nonconscious processes either dismiss moral responsibility or limit instances in which people are justifiably blameworthy or worthy of praise. He maintains that by adopting the consciousness thesis we need not be skeptical of desert-based moral responsibility since the consciousness condition can and often is met.

The criminal justice system has perhaps the best example of this in that it will determine before placing a person on trial for a crime whether there were any factors that made that person unaware that what they were doing was wrong. From a justice perspective, these factors could include severe mental illness, severe intoxication, or unintentional actions. This system, though, assumes that adult human beings are all aware of the most basic of crimes against another—murder, assault, theft, fraud, and the like. There cannot, therefore, be a defense from a mentally stable, otherwise normal, adult person that they were not aware that taking the life of another was wrong. While the criminal justice system does not use terms such as consciousness, it remains the basis of the responsibility question. If I commit an act that all adult human beings know to be wrong, then I am responsible for that act unless I can prove that I did not have consciousness of the wrongfulness of that act.

Levy's writings are part of an ever-growing school of thought that is addressing the link between morality and neuroscience. Part of this discussion is the consideration that although we may not be conscious of our motivations, we are still responsible for our actions if we have awareness around the wrongfulness of behaving that way.

This is therefore the dilemma we face when seeking to expand our consciousness. We will become better human beings, and more at peace, but we also gain a lot more responsibility for our actions. This is, of course, not a negative result but it is important to acknowledge. If you do not wish to accept responsibility for the things around which you have gained awareness, then do not begin a journey of expansion of consciousness. By the same token, in order to maintain an elevated state of consciousness, we should guard against taking responsibility for things that we cannot control. We should not allow our consciousness to be muddied by the energies of those who refuse to take responsibility for their actions. If responsibility is yours, accept it; if it is not, send it back out into the universe—it will eventually find its owner.

Conclusion

In *Understanding the Human Mind*, we have taken a journey through the concept of consciousness. We have explored the rise of consciousness and its evolution in the human brain, at least from a scientific point of view. Whether you align yourself with the scientific theories of the development of consciousness is completely up to you. It does leave us with some questions, though. If consciousness emanates in a specific area of the brain and only exists as a result of that organ, then does everything with a brain start out at the same level of consciousness? If so, what makes human beings able to develop a higher level of consciousness than animals, for instance? Or do animals actually have the same level of consciousness as humans and they simply express it differently? When exactly does consciousness form in a human being to the level that we should be responsible for our actions? Of course, the law has its own view on that but is it accurate?

How you view the information presented in this book will be completely up to your own view of the world. No two people will have the same experience of the information presented here, and each individual will place different weights on different sections. In reviewing what you have learned here, perhaps the very consideration of your experience of this book is an exercise in elevation of consciousness. Why did you place more weight on certain sections and less weight on others? What would change in your awareness if you allowed yourself to consider spiritual evidence as more weighty than scientific evidence or vice versa?

The debate around consciousness is quite an ironic one since we have only been engaged in this debate since we were aware of its existence. Although this debate has raged for a significant period of time, did we only start to debate it when we became aware or did we have a different type of awareness before that point and we have yet to come full circle?

Despite a myriad of explanations, the debate still rages on about what exactly consciousness is. Some believe it to mean that one is actively engaged with the sensory information that is being received and, therefore, one is aware of one's surroundings, feelings, thoughts, and sensations. This belief is a basic definition that in order to have consciousness, we must be awake and aware. Other groups believe that consciousness relies on the firing off of a large number of neurons in the brain. Those who take a more spiritual slant argue that consciousness is not dependent on any anatomical feature and that it is something that exists before we are born and after we die. Still, others believe that consciousness does not belong to an individual, and is, instead, something that we are tapping into that belongs to all of mankind.

As we have looked at the various philosophies around consciousness, one thing has become clear. No single philosophy holds all the answers. In fact, neither science, religion, spirituality, nor any other school of thought is capable of succinctly explaining the precise nature of consciousness and providing empirical evidence of these theories. Is this because none of these theories are correct, or is it because they are all correct in different ways?

Our understanding of consciousness must always begin with medical and scientific evidence. This is simply a factor of good critical thinking. MRI tests and other studies give us solid, factual evidence of where things happen in the brain and how our actions are affected by certain processes. This is important information, but it still doesn't answer all the questions. Scientists, doctors, psychologists, and neuroscientists will all acknowledge that even they do not fully understand human consciousness. Of course, this acknowledgment does not mean that we should discount any of their very valuable work on the subject, it simply means that there is more to be understood.

While religion or faith-based practices are not prominent in everyone's lives, they too provide an interesting and valid view on consciousness which cannot be discounted. Many people who follow organized religion or some form of spirituality often exhibit traits and behaviors that we would associate with existing on a higher level of consciousness. So surely there must be something to these practices?

Another irony around the pursuit of consciousness is that we seek a definitive answer. We want it to be black or white and find it difficult to accept that something as important as human consciousness might actually fall into a grey area. We want one school of thought or another to be proven ultimately correct and it to hold all of the answers to our questions. The simple fact is that this is never going to happen. Consciousness is a sum of so many different parts of our existence that we would actually be doing ourselves a great disservice by trying to pigeon-hole it into one theory or another. Perhaps the key to elevating our consciousness is not in defining it but rather in accepting and embracing its fluidity and other-worldliness.

By attempting to find the source, content, and workings of consciousness, we deny the most important factor of its existence—the magic of not knowing. Perhaps the questions that we still have around consciousness are meant to be unanswered, for now, in order to spur on our search for that knowledge. The very act of seeking the answers to our questions helps to elevate our consciousness, so it is certainly a journey we should continue on.

As you embark on this journey, be kind to yourself. Be aware of the self-limiting beliefs that we allow to weigh us down and rebuke them daily. You are not the sum of your past, and you are certainly not stuck in the state of consciousness that you now live. If there is one thing that we do know about consciousness, it is that it is constantly changing. Perhaps it is this fluidity that has caused our great challenges, as a species, in pinning it down, but it is definitely this changeable nature that we should celebrate. If our consciousness today does not have to be the same tomorrow as it is today, then the possibilities are endless.

The most likely scenario, looking at all of the various theories, philosophies, and schools of thought around consciousness, is that the truth about consciousness lies in an amalgamation of all of these things. How we piece together those answers may not be a group journey, but rather an individual one. Although our consciousness may be linked as a species, it is certainly still very individual and based on our own experiences, lenses, and biases. Therefore one perception of consciousness will never be the same as another, and, indeed, would we want it to be? Perhaps we don't need a final definition for consciousness? Maybe its definition is its changeable nature. The idea that we all see life through our own lenses is a very empowering one, because that means that you can change those lenses. Like a kaleidoscope, you can switch the lens and change your view. If you still struggle to accept that this theory of perceived reality is true, consider how you looked at life when you were 20 years old compared to how you look at it today. What has changed? Do you live on a different planet? Are you in a different body? No, of course not. The only thing that has changed is your perspective. Considering that perspective developed because of experiences that you went through, you can definitely create new experiences, a new perspective, and a new level of consciousness.

My hope for you, as you complete this book, is that you have gained a deeper understanding of the journey that humanity has taken, thus far, in exploring consciousness. This, of course, is your personal starting point and your own journey into exploring consciousness begins now. It is certainly important not to disregard any of the information you have gleaned from this book as that would be short-sighted. You cannot see your consciousness but you know it exists, so why would you use your five senses to limit your belief of anything else.

Personal growth is based on questioning your pre-existing beliefs. If you presume to know everything, then you are stuck in one place. Growth exists in acknowledging the gap in where we are now and where we would like to be, and working each and every day to get closer to the knowledge we seek. There is a huge amount of information in this book. If you need to, read through everything again, and when you do, focus more on the sections that made you uncomfortable in the first place. That is where you will grow the most. No one is asking you to believe things that you simply can't wrap your head around, but you should, at the very least, be willing to consider them.

When we acknowledge the fact that the answers we seek may be in all of the various schools of thought, we open ourselves up to growth. In this journey to understanding the human mind, perhaps we should celebrate the gaps, as in those gaps exists the opportunity to advance ourselves both individually and as a species.

References

Bayne, Tim, and Olivia Carter. *"Dimensions of Consciousness and the Psychedelic State."* Neuroscience of Consciousness, vol. 2018, no. 1, 1 Jan. 2018, www.ncbi.nlm.nih.gov/pmc/articles/PMC6146157/, 10.1093/nc/niy008.

Berlucchi, Giovanni, and Carlo Alberto Marzi. *"Neuropsychology of Consciousness: Some History and a Few New Trends."* Frontiers in Psychology, vol. 10, 30 Jan. 2019, 10.3389/fpsyg.2019.00050. Accessed 2 Dec. 2019.

"Brains of Smarter People Have Bigger and Faster Neurons - News." Www.Humanbrainproject.Eu, 21 Dec. 2018, www.humanbrainproject.eu/en/follow-hbp/news/brains-of-smarter-people-have-bigger-and-faster-neurons/.

Mandik, Pete. *"The Neurophilosophy of Consciousness."* The Blackwell Companion to Consciousness, 17 Mar. 2017, pp. 458–471, 10.1002/9781119132363.ch33. Accessed 8 July 2020.

McLeod, S. A. (2019, September 25). *Id, ego and superego.* Simply Psychology.

https://www.simplypsychology.org/psyche.html

www.ingramcontent.com/pod-product-compliance
Lightning Source LLC
Chambersburg PA
CBHW021442080526
44588CB00009B/644